Paul Arnott was born in publications such as the *In_____ ___ _____ *Time Out*, before becoming Series Editor of the Channel 4 daily arts programme. He has since evolved into a television producer and director, filming at Cannes, across India and Johannesburg and with the RSC.

A GOOD LIKENESS

PAUL ARNOTT

An *Abacus* Book

First published in Great Britain in 2000 by Little, Brown and Company
This edition published in 2001 by Abacus

A CIP catalogue record for this book
is available from the British Library.

ISBN 0 349 11328 9

Typeset in Horley Old Style by Palimpsest Book Production Limited,
Polmont, Stirlingshire
Printed and bound in Great Britain by
Clays Ltd, St Ives plc

Abacus
A division of
Little, Brown and Company (UK)
Brettenham House
Lancaster Place
London WC2E 7EN

www.littlebrown.co.uk

Contents

To my family

A Likeness

I DON'T KNOW where you are at the moment, but I'm three floors up in a back room of a well-worn Victorian house on top of a Lewisham hill, where I live with my wife, Lydia, our four children, and the sea of small troubles you might expect from someone overextended on just about every front. This is a room with an outlook over cabbage-leaf allotments that would have been part of our own garden before the First World War. To the west, where nightly I witness a fantastic pink and grey sunset in glorious cinema-scope, often traversed by a roaring Concorde heading for its early-evening landing at Heathrow, are the hills of south London, one of them topped by the tower of the Horniman Free Museum. When the trees are not in leaf and I look north-west I see the dome of St Paul's Cathedral, where last Christmas Day we bowled up on impulse for evensong, a rare observance and the first time I'd been under this dome since a visit to the Whispering Gallery as a lovesick schoolboy. I've come to love this house, because my family call it home, it's light, and it has a view you would never expect unless you had spent some years haunting one of inner London's least fancy boroughs. I deeply wish that we and not the mortgage company owned our home, and I fear I've spent so many years with a life built on shifting sand that I will never get a house built on rock, but maybe this will be the one. It was in this very room, as Jules Verne might have put it, that my adventure through time and space began.

Many people enliven their time on earth seeking adventure. By and large the ones available involve escaping from oneself, be it deep in the sea or high in the sky or shooting ink pellets at one another across a coppice. That kind of adventure is a buzz, and after it's been experienced its benefit lies in the pure surge of self-awareness elicited by a battle against the odds. What happened to me seems a rarer type. It was an unsought adventure, where every day took me closer to the full awareness of a parallel life I could have led, taking me on a journey back through time where all of the protagonists were alive and longing to tell me what I'd missed, precisely at a moment in history where the hypocrisies, deceits and misadventures of a dying moral order are receiving the coup de grace.

It's an adventure that, I have come to believe, came into my life at just the point where the characteristic endurance and stoicism of an adopted son was in danger of curdling into paralysis and self-denial. I could not have lived through a more purely amazing passage of time if I had been swept into the pages of a *Harry Potter* book. Later on I will mention the names of some notable adopted figures, but as I've been reading a nightly chapter of *Harry Potter* to my two sons recently I've found that of all the adopted literary and historical figures around, he is the only one with whom I really connect – a boy unknowingly born from wizard stock, scarred in instinctive battle against the forces of darkness, and raised in Privet Drive before slowly, awkwardly and without delusion being drawn to the real-isation of who he really is.

Mine became a tale I was prompted to tell many times in the months that followed my discoveries, and at the end of many evenings a departing guest would invariably say, 'Do you know, this would make a great book?' As my wife closed the door behind them I would invariably loftily say, 'Not in a million years' or 'Why does everything today have to be turned into a bloody book?'

My resistance to writing a single sentence hardened after an evening with an Australian friend, my only schoolmate to have made not one but two fortunes, the latter in market-ing. Eyes bulging, he gripped the table and said, 'Christ, mate, you're a marketing man's dream. The thing my creatives know about commercials is that the ones that sell the product are always based in a truth-based proposition.' I'm very fond of my Australian mate (perhaps his eyes didn't actually bulge), and I even have respect for his ability to market Chicken Tonight ('Chicken TONIGHT!'), but could I be led by such a self-serving view of the world?

Then, one Friday evening about a year ago, I was sitting watching *Frasier* when something knife-like in my abdomen seemed to be carving a new exit to the outside world. Lydia confidently, even derisively – for modern man lacks a reputation for bearing pain with the other sex – diagnosed acute constipation and fetched a homeopathic pill. I swallowed it to save a debate on alternative medicine, but a night spent squirming on the floor saying, 'Oh God,' and 'Aaaagh,' indicated that on this occasion a teeny arsenicum pill from the Helios Box of 36 Basic Homeopathic Remedies was not going to do the trick.

The pain was so excruciating that I was truly grateful the next lunchtime, when I was finally allowed to go to our superb family doctor, Dr McNair, who became the first of four physicians to rummage in my bottom that day. Having disposed of her rubber glove she phoned the hospital and told them to sharpen their scalpels: an appendix was about to blow.

At about teatime I found myself on a trolley wearing a green, paperette, backless slip in a south London hospital, looking up at the Teletubbies posters that I'd so often shown to one of the children as they had had bits of our garden removed from their foreheads. It was a Saturday, and as I was wheeled into the anaesthetist's room outside the operating theatre I wondered if statistics showed that Saturday afternoon was either a very good or a very bad time to have emergency surgery. Both anaesthetists were masked and it was hard to tell who was the main man. When one of them said to the other, 'Er . . . I mean *fifty* mills . . .' 'You said *five* . . .' 'Yeah, sorry, I've been on since last night,' my thoughts turned to my own mortality. It dawned upon me that for the first time since my whole adoption story had begun I was about to be rendered completely unconscious.

What, I wondered as the anaesthetist began to pump the morphine into my drip, if she was delivering too large a dose? What if she'd initially trained as a vet and was sending through enough knockout drops for a rhinoceros? What if this antechamber to the operating theatre was to be the place of my last ever thoughts? What, in short, if I was about to die?

I apologise if my three last thoughts before unconsciousness seem in some way shallow. Thought One, whose rigid upper lip really astonished me, was: 'I don't really want to go now, but if I do it hasn't been a bad knock.' Even as that banal thought ebbed away I realised I should be grateful for it, reassured that if this was a dry run for my eventual real death then how wonderful that I might not be one of those who rage against the dying of the light.

With twenty seconds to oblivion, however, Thought Two crashed into this complacent reverie. 'Hang on, you moron,' it reasoned, 'you've got a wife and four children. And the oldest is only seven. You must, must make it through this operation. They actually, tangibly need you. So shape up, you self-satisfied buffoon.' I was in no condition to make any shape other than beached whale, but I instantly sent a robust email to my heart and lungs, apologising for recent neglect and proposing that if they pressed on through the current crisis I'd readdress their recent complaints on my return to work.

Ten seconds to go, and I was still thinking about our children. And I think, not for the first time, that in many ways time may prove them to be the greatest beneficiaries of my adoption quest, that they are now plugged into a network of cousins, aunts and uncles and a different nation they would otherwise not have known. And then I had Thought Three, and it really disturbed me: If I did fail to awake from this operation, my children would never know that under the surface I believed my adoption trail, from its accidental beginning five years before to the joy of attending my natural sister's wedding a year later, had been for me no less than a series of unlooked-for epiphanies. Worse still, while they could get fragments of what had happened to me from the various parties involved, the only person who had seen and still held the map for the whole area was me. The thought of my children seeking out the truth of my story a couple of decades hence and being sent quite benignly in the wrong direction was actually repellent. Right, I thought. I won't lose consciousness for this operation, and if I can feel the knife then so be it. The deal is that if I make it through alive I will acknowledge my responsibility to write the story down.

Then I passed out.

1

First, Marinade

How could my timings have gone so wrong? When I'd read my one-man adaptation of *Jack and the Beanstalk* aloud to myself on the morning of Jake's third birthday party, the running time was just over ten minutes. Three words per second is the rule of thumb in writing scripts for newsreaders, the nearest thing broadcasting has to an invariable.

When, however, I gave my performance that September afternoon I found myself twenty long minutes in with Jack still stealing golden eggs from under the giant's nose, and with at least another ten minutes still to go before he'd axe the beanstalk to the earth. And as the show ground on I had the leisure to repent its grave flaws. Lydia had done a lovely job converting the cardboard box in which our refrigerator had been delivered into a Punch-and-Judy-style theatre, but it soon became apparent that I should have found a stool to sit on rather than kneeling on our thinly carpeted floor. Neither was it a masterstroke to compound this by manipulating an unrehearsed cast of Jake's toys with my hands above my head for half an hour. My forearms, which at first merely burned like a martyr's smock, were now losing all sensation, as the searing waves of pain migrated to the small of my back, where they were joined in a pit of perspiration by messages of torment shooting up from my kneecaps.

Worse still, I was not, as they say, off the script, which is to say that I was entirely dependent on being able to read what I had written. The only way of doing this was to put the script in front of my knees on the floor and, with arms still aloft moving Little Ted across the stage, crane my neck down for a glimpse of this increasingly epic adaptation. Seen in profile, I probably resembled a Samurai's victim making honourable preparation for his own execution.

The other main flaw was my choice of material. For the amateur children's entertainer, there are few laughs in *Jack and the Beanstalk*. True, Jack begins as a complete idiot, and there's some mileage to be had when his mother realises he has sold their cow for a handful of beans, but thereafter Jack's story is like a dry run for *Die Hard* – all climbing, stealing, fleeing and chopping, with Jack becoming something of a hard man in the denouement.

Therefore, sealed in my fridge box, unable to see my audience, starved of any textual excuses to make them laugh, and beginning to spasm with back pain, I began to get a bit paranoid. Rather like the giant, in the silence I was no longer sure whether there was anyone else in the room with me. Were Jake and his three-year-old chums riveted by every word on the other side of the painted cardboard, or had they gradually slipped away into the kitchen for chocolate fingers and then made a dash for the garden, where even now they were concluding a round of pass the parcel?

But the advantage of paranoia is that, like thinking about goals one might score on a rainy walk to the railway station, it distracts the conscious mind and seems to make time pass faster. Before I knew it Little Ted had hacked the twig and cotton wool that represented the beanstalk to the clouds and I was saying, 'And so Jack lived happily ever after.' With applause ringing in my ears, I crawled out of the back of the fridge box, slowly walked myself up an armchair to the perpendicular and, like Donald Wolfit at the stage door of Drury Lane, swept from behind the box to accept the praise of the assembled parents, many of whom were truly grateful that I had managed to get their three-year-olds to nap peacefully on the carpet. Fortunately Jake, who has always had a rapacious appetite for plays and books, was still staring at the little stage. He would probably have hung around to watch his toys encore *Waiting for Godot*.

If I'd been a professional I would then have blown up a few balloons in the shape of a giraffe, had a hundred quid pressed into my hand by a grateful dad, told a tipsy young mum about my forthcoming *Hamlet* at the Man in the

Moon and fled the premises. As an amateur, however, I had another major role left to play, one not best suited to a man with a tremor in his arms and a body twitching like a Bacofoiled marathon runner on Westminster Bridge. While Lydia plied the parents with drink, which on this Indian summer afternoon seemed to be going straight to their heads, I had to barbecue a hundredweight of chicken legs together with fat fistfuls of bespoke sausages from O'Hagan's Sausage Shop in Greenwich.

Like my *Jack*, from my high hopes of the morning the sausages were to become something of a disappointment. By buying from O'Hagan's we were supporting the feeble pulse of culinary culture south of the river Thames. O'Hagan could give you a standard banger, but how could one emerge from his shop with half a pound of these rather than his Venison and Greengage, Mulberry and Swordfish, Veal and Plum? All with very little ballast and 'encased in natural skins'.

With children about, and overeducated parents, even in their cups, looking on from the health and safety perspective, priority number one with the chicken had to be the prevention of someone biting into a drumstick only for their canines to emerge stained with chilled blood. I aimed to give each leg at least twenty minutes, flick the ones that had turned to charcoal over the fence into the allotments, and then finesse the remainder for another ten before serving. By now the children were already stuffed with biscuits and crisps, but the adult take-up was astonishing and could only be explained by their drink-impaired judgement.

But oh, my sausages. They had undergone an identical regimen to the chicken, when what they really required was about half the cooking time and a lot of one-on-one care. Really, they only had themselves to blame. It was all very well O'Hagan's selling Ox and Gorgonzola, but why didn't they tell you these things still contained animal fat, bubbling matter that oozed ceaselessly on to the coals below to create an even more intense flame? By the time I had managed to give the sausages the attention they craved, all that was left was the natural skin, which was, as one might have expected, extremely realistic, suggesting that its true purpose might actually have been as something else for the weekend.

I feel these things deeply. Behind a jovial facade I felt that both *Jack* and the sausages had flopped, and that I was the only person at the party not having a fantastically good time. As I squeezed back indoors through the kitchen I encountered an old friend, Claire. As cub reviewers, we had spent much of our late twenties writing about the extremities of London's fringe theatre. Given my insecurity about the range and depth of my *Jack* and the budding critical intelligence of her three-year-old, Arthur, I was keen to brush straight past her. But Claire was laughing hysterically, pointing at the floor and at me, chuckling, 'It's absolutely extraordinary. He's you. He's just a little you. Can't you see it?'

She was pointing at our second son, Benjamin, whose first birthday was three weeks away. He was pulling himself up at Claire's feet by grasping the kitchen table ready to make another attempt at walking.

'Paul, he could be you. It's almost as if you've been shrunk. Hahahahaha.'

'Hahaha,' I replied, quick as a flash, and moved on through the sitting-room door towards the staircase, intent on escape. If there'd been a substitute father on the bench I'd have brought him on, but as it was I knew that I could only survive the rest of the afternoon if I stole a few moments' time out.

I suppose ninety-nine per cent of the quarter of a million trips you make up your staircase in a lifetime are purely functional. Some ascents, though, at critical moments, seem to be much more than that. By the time I'd reached my little office at the top of the house I was no longer the same man who had started the climb half a minute before.

It must be inconceivable, to those raised by their blood parents, surrounded by grandparents, sisters and brothers, that a man in his thirties had never given any serious credit to the potency of family resemblance. I must seem like a man with a missing dimension, almost as if one had stumbled across a throwback who had never developed a sense of smell. Yet just as someone unable to sense the aroma of cut grass or madeleines soon adapts without any conscious effort, so I had spent all this time in a haze of unknowing, oblivious to the importance of any link connecting my looks with those of another human being. Of course I realised that Kirk and Michael Douglas had the same cleft chin and ground teeth, but as an area of discussion it didn't seem to bother me. It could all have been different if I had been an Aborigine adopted by the Svenssons of Stockholm, but in suburban south London I looked sufficiently like my mum, dad and older brother for it never to develop into an issue. My dad was over six feet tall, with a fetching 'tache and trim sideburns of the Stewart Granger ilk, and big blue eyes. Although he was already forty-two when I was adopted, I considered him quite a blade, and if I wanted to grow up to look like anyone, it was him. Possessed of eyes just like his, I felt as if I was already part of the way there.

From an early age I'd behaved like the *Beano*'s Billy Whizz, and this paid off occasionally on the athletics track. During my childhood I was forever racing our cocker spaniel up the road, leaping on to the back platform of departing Routemasters, and running after family guests in their Austin 1100s until they joined the traffic on the A21. It all seemed to add up – my mum had been a sprint champion at school and my brother, not otherwise attracted to sport, was a regular finalist in the 100 metres on sports day. As a standard-issue nuclear family, even though none of us were related by blood, we made perfect visual sense, and in that we were probably very lucky. I remember my mum saying that some of my facial expressions were like her father's, who died when I was six. I thought he was terrific and had no problem with this, while for my mother it was possibly an enormous comfort that I might be taking something from her family line, even if this might only have been an understandable projection on her part which lacked much supporting evidence.

One of the characteristics I developed as an adopted child was a profound scepticism. But this scepticism co-existed with an opposite tendency – an unshakeable respect for the views of a small number of people who'd struck me as being both perceptive and purposeful, who seemed inherently inclined towards insight and fairness. When they casually uttered something that I sensed was nothing short of an eternal verity, my world stopped revolving for a few seconds. It could be years later before I fully grasped why whatever they had just said had such massive significance. Claire was one of these people who made my ears prick up.

When I reached the top of the stairs I threw my sodden baseball cap on to a chair and, with the party going on perfectly happily without me, sat behind my desk for a few moments of reflection. She's right, I thought, Benjamin is like me. And I could see why it made her laugh, too. When Jake was a baby everyone said he was my spitting image. He had big blue eyes and, naturally, looked like a baby. Even by his first birthday, though, his mother's bone structure (a characteristic for which I had been denied the genetic code) was coming through, and he was becoming a fine-looking chap from Lydia's line. I, on the other hand, still looked like an overgrown baby.

The reason for this, and really the most enormous clue if only I'd known as to my true national origin, is that I have a big head. I like to think that I have a normal head, and it would top off a man of seven feet, two inches rather well, but at five feet, ten inches there is no denying that it gives me a certain presence when I walk into a room. It's also a roundish head, rather than one of those high Frankenstein jobs. Whether this means that I represent the next stage in man's evolution, a superskull containing an ultrabrain with the power of a mainframe computer, or whether those pinheaded people are actually the next stage with their compressed microchip layouts on a laptop scale, I am not sure. Although one might note that there always seems to be something that a laptop simply can't do.

Benjamin's hat size will not, I believe, inflate quite to my proportions. But when he went on the Pirate Falls log flume ride at Legoland Windsor, sitting in front of Lydia, an unexpectedly sudden plunge down a chute made him fly backwards, planting the back of his head against her lip and nose. She looked as if she'd been hit in the face by one of those demolition balls and, after bleeding copiously over a scale model of Copenhagen, had to be offered first aid.

The fact that Claire would always think of me as the man with an extra portion of head on his shoulders was what made her laugh when confronted by the attempts to walk of this plucky little eleven-month-old, whose shoulders she saw were destined also to have extra weight to bear. But the effect of her throwaway line, my mind softened up by the stress of Jack and the sausages, was the disorientating equivalent to being presented with that perception-study picture that looks like a vase, and then like two faces, no it's a vase, hang on, it's definitely two faces. While she had given me an entirely fresh premise – 'If Benjamin looks like me then I look like someone else' – she had also caused a vase–face perception problem, in which my cortex fizzed with two competing and incompatible concepts of my humanity. Either it was extraordinarily vital that I had begun a train of thought that would lead inevitably to contemplation of the possibility of another living being, one who had gone before me, to whom I might be fully connected by blood, or yielding primacy to the importance of facial and physical resemblances really was feeble-minded, vain and a lazy approach to man's identity. One road might lead to another being, the other would deliber-ately blow itself up.

I stood and walked from behind my desk out on to the tiny roof terrace that looks out over our garden. The only stone-cold sober adult at the party, I was gazing down on the figures below, one of whom was Lydia. As I gazed at the top of her head I tried to imagine for a moment what she would have felt, what we would have felt, if we had quite simply mislaid one of our children. Devastated. Would we ever forget this child? No, we would not.

Perhaps there was a woman somewhere out there who gave birth to me in adverse circumstances in 1961, gave me up for adoption, and who all these years later regretted her decision. A woman who, I realised, in English law had no chance of ever hearing what became of that baby unless the man that baby had become made an active decision to trace her. On the other hand, there could be some utter old bag who, having been knocked up by a sailor, threw me at the midwife, left hospital and died a few months later of an overdose of heroin. The face and the vase competed for my perception.

The decision I would make as I turned back into the room was self-evidently taken mainly because of the kind of person I was. I sat back down and did a ludicrous scribble with cartoons of three of the heroes of my developmental years, Captain Scarlet, Captain Kirk and Captain Mainwaring. All of them were, sometimes foolishly but always romantically, determined to do the right thing. Scarlet had been a perfect puppet hero for a child, both prepubescent and immortal. Kirk was ideal for the teenager, because he was either being flogged or snogged. Mainwaring became my hero as a young adult when I realised that appearing to be a buffoon and having your heart in the right place often went hand in hand.

What if these three captains had strategised with me in my office HQ this hot afternoon? Scarlet's counsel I would have ignored, I think, since his contingency plan for any course of action, his own death, seemed unattractive and over the top in the circumstances. Kirk might have cited Spock, who endured perpetual inner conflict between his Vulcan logic and the subversion of his flickering human emotions. Mainwaring would have watched them both with that fabulous sense of exasperation and ordered me to proceed with extreme caution. What Mainwaring would not have done was turn back.

I had to take a best guess, what the business traveller calls a judgement call. Based on the little that I knew back then, I understood most adoption arose out of illegitimacy. But since my own adoption in 1961 the stigma attached to illegitimacy had almost completely eroded. What if this hypothetical woman, who had made and carried me, had been one of the thousands who fell victim to the prejudices of her day? Wasn't it up to me, in this information age, at least to write her a letter, a letter that said I was alive? The reception this letter met with couldn't be my primary concern. If it was screwed up and put in the bin then I'd done my bit. And if it wasn't? I had no idea, but surely a woman whose line had led to my own two wonderful sons couldn't have been all bad. Looking at them, it seemed hard to conceive that she could be bad at all.

I love my children with all my heart, but I know that one day their respect for me will not be unconditional. They will know by the age of eighteen whether I have been a good or a bad father. But what if I slipped under a bus when they were teenagers, say, and had the opportunity of only a few last words. What if one of them said to me, 'Daddy, who were your natural parents?' and the only reply I could muster was, 'I don't know. I couldn't be bothered to find out.' In my death I would be finally obliterating not only my own roots but also theirs. As well, perhaps, as the hopes of this hypothetical woman. And I like to think that if I had done nothing and my children had one day given it some thought they would have judged that by doing nothing I had allowed myself to become complicit in one of the twentieth century's more serious social injustices.

From downstairs I heard someone saying goodbye and remembered that neither of us had sliced up the birthday cake for the going-away bags. Once again I was confronted by the failings of a grand scheme, for the cake was a boxed Sainsbury's job, the kind of immortal confection you could bury and dig up a year later in perfectly preserved condition. It was a late substitute for a Captain Scarlet cake I had attempted to make; it had not risen a single millimetre, having choked on the blue and red food colouring that I had whisked in, convinced that Spectrum's logo could be reproduced in cake form. The poor thing never had a chance.

When I got downstairs I saw Claire, and I studied her Poohishly to see if she was aware of the epiphany she had just caused. She, of course, had no inkling. It was an early and clear indication that in a matter such as this, wherever it led, I could only have myself to blame.

If you are a person who was adopted in England before 1975 your birth certificate will be about half the normal size. It's rather as if you'd missed out on the School Cup, with its engraved list of winning names stretching back years, and had been given one of those consolation

Certificates of Merit for Good Behaviour. Better than nothing, possible to frame, but compared to the cup absolutely meaningless.

What you are after, therefore, if you are an adopted person who wants to trace your natural parents, is the full-size birth certificate, which will list the names and addresses (at your time of birth) of your natural mother and quite possibly your natural father. Obviously this piece of paper is loaded with an extraordinary weight of emotional and historical significance. This does not mean, however, that the early stages of locating it are in any way interesting. Going to Tashkent, now that's interesting, but you can't do it without a passport, the application process for which is deadly dull. Acquiring the freedom of the road aged seventeen, that's a modern miracle, but one's travails applying to the DVLC in Swansea for a conditional driving licence are just paperwork.

In initially tracking down my original birth certificate I was drawn inevitably towards the home of all English birth records, St Catherine's House on Aldwych in London. On the Monday after Jake's birthday I rang them up and they sent me a leaflet that advised me that I would have to undertake counselling before I would be allowed to search for my birth certificate. This could be done, if I wished, through the local social services or through the adoption society (if any) through which my adoption had been arranged. It also said that there was a National Contact Register where, if both birth parent and adopted child registered their names, it might be possible to help put the two parties in touch, although the failure of either of those parties to register would render the other's interest impotent.

Those two words – social . . . services. On the one hand, one of the maturer mothers at Jake's school, with whom I would trust my life, is an inner London social worker specialising in adoption, a fascinating and kind woman, deeply unhappy with some of the foolishness of her own department and fighting for common sense from within. On the other hand, a woman I studied psychology with at university is now also a social worker and she had struck me, I'm afraid, as just the kind of weak personality who would drink in every word of politically correct lunacy she would have been told at conferences over more than a decade and make ideal casting in *The Crucible*.

I was keenly aware that this would be the first time in my entire life that I'd speak about my adoption and my feelings about it to a professional person. I suppose I decided that I would not want to see a social worker because I wanted the freedom to say the outrageous, if I wished, without it being duly noted. It became clear in my mind that if I could manage to arrange it I would prefer to go first by the adoption society route. If the society still existed and there was an old case file, it might be the only place left with any colour or detail about this hypothetical mother.

My next stop then (and I did warn you) was the *Yellow Pages*. As a child I remember my mother and father getting regular correspondence from an organisation called the Phyllis Holman Richards Adoption Society. Obviously I didn't read it, but I remember thinking it was brazen of the society to get our postman to stuff letters through the front door with their franked identity splashed all over it. If the whole business was a secret, which it was, it was about as indiscreet as sending porn through the post in a cellophane wrapper. There's a bastard living here, Postie. But all these years later I suppose I was fortunate that Mrs Richards had such a memorable name, one that had stuck in the mind of a child.

The *Yellow Pages* revealed that the Phyllis Holman Richards Adoption Society was no longer based in Belgravia, but was now found in Wandsworth. I phoned. At this earliest of stages I was cautious about getting carried away by the drama of the events I was initiating, yet undeniably it seemed deeply portentous even to be speaking to someone at the adoption society. The receptionist seemed to know very well that she was exercising a role that often brought her close to the fertile, dangerous world of human secrets.

Nevertheless, my query was simply stated and meant to yield only a factual response of policy. 'I believe your agency may have been involved in my adoption and I would like to know what the procedure is in finding out more.' The receptionist advised me to write in, which I duly did as soon as I had put the phone down, much as one might write for details of membership schemes from the local gym. What I fully expected in reply was to be sent a leaflet in the style of the one from St Catherine's House. The letter I wrote on 7 September, three days after Jake's birthday, was remarkable only for its mealy-mouthed neutrality.

I am writing to you requesting assistance in discovering information concerning my adoption in 1961, which your society arranged. I understand that you are kind enough to offer a counselling service for adopted children like me and I would like to put myself forward for this procedure, with a view to possibly (and only possibly) taking the process of tracing my natural parents a little further.

I imagined that this was an appropriately neutral, Majorite tone, and it seemed clear to me that I was asking for an initial counselling meeting, which might then be followed, after I'd had more time to think, by my being given some of the information in their files. With my hand on my heart I had not expected the following letter to drop through our letterbox on a Saturday morning a week and a half later:

Dear Mr Arnott
Thank you for your letter dated 7th September.
Our records from the period of your adoption are rather brief but I can give you a little information about your natural parents.
Your natural parents were a married couple, both Irish and Roman Catholic, living and working in England. Your

natural mother was a SRN, and your father was an engin-
eer, welder and fitter. Your natural mother was 22 years old
at the time of your birth, 5' 5" tall with dark hair and blue
eyes. Her interests were musical. Your natural father was 30
years old, 5' 10" tall with brown hair and blue eyes. He was
interested in sport and athletics. They both enjoyed good
health. The name they gave you was Rory. The reason given
for placing you for adoption was that they could not have
afforded to keep a baby. They lived in a rented room and were
in financial difficulties.

If you decide that you would like to try to trace your natural
family I will be happy to meet with you for the necessary
counselling. Please telephone to arrange an appointment.

You will also need to apply for access to your original birth
certificate and the enclosed leaflet gives information about
this.

It was signed by the director of the adoption agency.

It was as if out of the blue an atheist had received a letter
from God confirming in no uncertain terms that He did
indeed exist and would look forward to seeing him in
church on Sunday. I think I looked, that Saturday morning,
like one looks in the first flush of a passionate affair, as if
I'd connected my face to the National Grid.

We were due to spend the weekend with some friends,
Martin and Miranda, in a rickety outhouse in the grounds
of Miranda's father's grand pile, Watlington Hall. We

usually spend our weekends at McDonald's, but fortunately this Saturday we were living high on the hog. As we drove through London and out on the M40 I held the letter on the steering wheel and read it over and over again. When we came through that famous gap in the Chilterns where you suddenly see Oxfordshire stretching out before you, I felt as if with one more push on the accelerator we could fly straight over it like Peter Pan. That we were staying at a place called Christmas Common seemed to intensify this sense of magic.

Showing Martin and Miranda the letter felt like revealing a winning lottery ticket, or a gold bar that had been slipped anonymously through the letterbox. Something very strange was happening. The section of my mind concerned with the concept of identity, which had been lying under a sheet in the garage since I was born, suddenly roared into life. I found myself seeing Martin not as a young city solicitor spattered with children but as someone who would want you to know and understand his identity.

Martin and I were alike in two senses; we seemed unable to use contraception and we were both carrying a few extra pounds (all right, stones). For some reason we did a manly thing that I hardly ever do, which was to go to the pub before lunch. There, Martin related how the carapace of his daily identity (Winchester, Oxford, law – and frankly not too hard to spot this either) had two much more powerful undercurrents – his Cornishness, which I had known about, and his Jewishness, which I had not. Cornish he looks, and he would grace any remake of *Poldark*. He looks about as Jewish, however, as Mao Tse-tung, and yet this was the scab that he really wanted to pick.

As he told me all this he drained at least four pint glasses in about half an hour, and I managed three of the local cider. For me this is rollercoaster stuff, and as he drove us back through the woods I begged him to stop. I tumbled out of the car and the cider exploded out of me against a rather fine mountain ash. For the first time since Jake had been born I was properly and deliriously out of control and I leaned back against a tree and laughed. The two of them had been right.

Gilly, a milliner I once knew (whom I suspect was only interested in me to see if she could make a hat big enough), had been educated at Trinity College, Dublin and been out with an Irish boxer with dubious nationalist connections. One day she had said without any doubt, 'You do know you're Irish, don't you?' Which I didn't know how to take. What, Liam Neeson sort of Irish? Or Daniel O'Donnell? I never got an answer.

And my best friend, Cris. We'd played a football match a few years earlier on Blackheath against Dynamo Digbeth, and in the Princess of Wales pub afterwards I found myself in a centrally placed chair being friendly with the opposition. I had no idea what the craic was then but I suppose I was making it, fraternising with the enemy, being pointlessly happy. Cris was a junior barrister, a new tenant in chambers, and was in an early Shavian phase where he

found it hard to suppress the odd mildly pompous assess-
ment of character. Rather rudely, I thought, he set down
his glass and blurted out, 'Has anyone ever compared you
to Terry Wogan?' Given that on my twenty-first birthday
he had sent me a copy of F. Scott Fitzgerald's *Tender Is the
Night* inscribed, 'See if you are aware of any comparisons',
I couldn't quite grasp how he felt Dick Diver had deteri-
orated into Terry Wogan in less than five years. But I knew
what he meant.

The large house in Wandsworth where the adoption society
is now located doesn't seem to do much business anymore.
At the front downstairs there is still a mother and baby
room, but these days an illegitimate conception is either
unproblematic or terminated before it grows into a noticeable problem. It would be most unfair to suggest that the
building was in some sense spooky or covered in cobwebs,
but it certainly had the tang of a place where many young
mothers might once have been parted from their babies in
circumstances they might have a lifetime to regret. I felt
like a Dickensian character whose fortunes are about to be
transformed by a meeting with a distinguished personage.
    The director of the society was elegant and courteous,
and like many of those who've grown up speaking English
away from its motherland spoke with some of the most
elegant structure and precision I had heard in some time.
She was from Durban originally. Earlier in the year I had
done some filming in Johannesburg and a nearby township

for a programme about the community work of the Market
Theatre, and I'd interviewed some people that interested
her, particularly the playwright Athol Fugard. It seemed
reassuring not only that we had something to talk about
that wasn't the main meal, but that here was a person I felt
naturally in sympathy with.

It was just ten days after I had received her letter. My
first question on the matter at hand was to ask why she had
given me so much detail in her reply, when I had quite
clearly expressed only a most undeveloped interest. She
replied that the society tended to do that because if individuals in my position were given it straight up it either
made them freeze in their tracks or, more likely, beat their
way to the society's door with real commitment. I found
her reply only partially convincing, but I guessed that
behind it was some careful consideration of policy and a
commitment to greater openness. Also a realism: someone
who had gone as far as writing a letter probably intended
and desired deep down to pursue their quest.

We both drew breath. The reason I was there could no
longer be avoided. To my mild relief she didn't seem
particularly concerned about grilling me at length as to
my preparedness for an adoption quest. I think it was
pretty obvious that I fell slapbang into the category of
questers who only decide to search after they have a well-
developed family of their own, where in effect they have
a secure new life and nothing to lose. A new line has been
established and they are at its head – even the rankest of

rejections, while unwelcome, would only be a temporary setback.

When she opened the slim file, however, I feared for a moment that she might be about to disappoint me, for her opening line was almost tragicomic.

'My task has not been an easy one,' she began. 'Phyllis Holman Richards died some years ago, and when she was compiling your file she was in the latter stages of Parkinson's disease. Much of what she has written is, to be honest with you, cryptic.'

I fully expected her to close the manila folder, wish me well and show me to the door.

'However,' she continued, 'I have managed to piece some of the story together.' She told me that the young Irish couple were a Mr and Mrs Brennan, from an unspecified part of rural Ireland, both from farming backgrounds. They had been married for four months when I was born but had been friends for three years. Nobody in their families knew of the pregnancy, and in those days the obvious failure for the date of marriage and the date of birth to tally would have been a cause of considerable disgrace. She didn't know where they were married, whether in Ireland or England, or where they went after my adoption.

Mr Brennan worked as an engineer's fitter and his family engineering company had gone bust. Mrs Brennan was studying for the final stages of her nursing exams at St Giles's Hospital, Camberwell. It may have been that these exams and the birth were combined on the same trip.

All of this detail I wrote down carefully, knowing that later I would want to digest it, unable to both write and register its impact simultaneously. What the director told me next, however, made me stop dead and ask for her to say it again. 'At the time of your birth they lived at 48 Lee Terrace, Blackheath.'

I have spent the last fifteen years living either in or near Blackheath, and Lee Terrace is less than a mile from my home. I have always loved Blackheath and Greenwich, and although I had lived previously in a number of places within reach of many Londoners' favourite open space, Hampstead Heath, I had always found the blasted Blackheath and its sister, the astronomers' park, infinitely more compelling. Perhaps it is that the two together give a sense of a plateau above London, with the glorious effect at the escarpment in Greenwich Park of the earth plunging away to the valley of the Thames below. Unlike a trip up the stairs, a walk from my house to Greenwich across Blackheath always releases fresh thought, or enables a complex problem to acquire a sense of proportion. And this walk always takes me along Lee Terrace. And the drive across the Heath to Greenwich Hospital had been our last trip before both Jake and Benjamin were born, Jake's trip in bright sunshine in the morning rush hour, Benjamin's under the stars just before midnight.

At this point I began to see one of the benefits of the director's doubtless difficult job, moments such as these when she was able to create and then witness a little spark of magic in someone else's life. With the news of the Blackheath connection the utter intangibility of these strangers, these Irish people, faded a little. Whoever they were and whatever their problems, they had chosen a fantastic place to have their romance.

There were three more details left in the file. Immediately after the birth the baby had been given over to a foster parent, a Mrs Dubber in Purley, and was then handed over to its new parents after three weeks, the delay having been caused because the baby was having trouble feeding. Then there was a letter on file from A.M. Brennan (Mrs) saying she was pleased that the baby had gone to a good home, and finally a letter from my father saying that everyone in Bromley was very pleased with me and thanking the society again.

The director and I talked for another twenty minutes or so. For the first time I realised that I was one of a breed of people whom she might encounter every now and then who were effectively irrelevant to the contemporary work of an adoption society. The age of the discreet birth in conditions of confinement followed by an assignment of rights over the baby to a respectable family is over. Adoption is much more complicated than that today. And yet for over fifty years from the end of the First World War to 1975, when the English law changed allowing adopted children to have access to their birth records, there were as many as 25,000 people adopted in precisely this way every year. That's around three-quarters of a million

half-size birth certificates still in circulation, and a hell of
a lot of secrets. The numbers in the United States, where
the figure for adoptions was nearer 175,000 per annum,
are off the scale. And in America there are only three states
where a citizen has the right, as we do in England, to get
hold of this original birth certificate. That's a hell of a lot
of suppressed secrets.

When I returned home from Wandsworth I kept writing.
Ten years before, as a twenty-two-year-old, I had what is
known as a doomed affair. Only years later did I realise
that practically everyone has a doomed affair in their
twenties, but at the time, with my partner in doom being
engaged to someone else and the high drama of it all, it did
seem like doom squared, cubed. Luckily during this affair
a wafer-thin slice of frontal lobe activity had told me, 'This
will come to an end. Write it down.' So I had done, almost
daily as the affair progressed, and when after six months it
ended and I plunged to my doom, the green folder with
dozens of pages of reportage from the trenches of impas-
sioned self-destruction were comfort squared, cubed, probably because in the very first pages there was a reminder
of a person I still recognised, whom I realised in time I
would become again.

Following that example of getting it all down, this is
precisely what I wrote back at my desk after the visit to the
adoption society:

To my surprise there were only two elements which really touched me at this stage. The letter from my father depicted a kind man at his best, a part of whom is still present but which is too often twisted with some deep and unspecifiable anger with life.

The more significant emotion was a feeling in me of a sorrow for a generation of Irish people who were too poor to keep their own kids and had to give them away to people in England. That both societies had become so dysfunctional, so cold, that they could countenance the giving away of one's own kin for reasons of economic hardship. There is no one to blame in this – it is just a continuing part of the human tragedy, that I have to look at Jake or Benjamin to see any continuity in what it means to have been born me, and that I had always denied myself a genuine emotional identification with my parents because I always knew in my heart that they were not me.

Indeed, I think my mother often took the workhouse view that I was naturally flawed like those two poor copulating paddies, and this made her ridiculously, often cruelly and unnaturally, on the look-out for the emergence of some degenerance in me – the me who has been Captain Sensible from day one, precisely because my inauspicious beginning gave me a massive hint that life was not to be trusted, and that if you didn't look after yourself nobody else would.

There seems little point in berating myself for the woodenness of this writing, or in attempting to analyse the repressions, denials, projections and God knows what else can be deduced. It's pretty clear that I had passed through the mirror, out of the land where I felt I could right an injustice and into the land where it was impossible for me to resist the lure of further understanding. I've since read dozens of other anecdotal accounts of adoption quests, mainly American, and as an Englishman on first reading them I found some of them pretty repulsive, egomaniac, who-am-I?, why-was-I-betrayed? masterpieces of undiluted whinging, often giving a principal role to an expensive therapist called Wanda, for whose plight at having to listen to this stuff one felt a deep sympathy.

Yet reading now, several years on, the words that I wrote after my return from Wandsworth, I realise that I was no different from them. Yes, there were bad deeds that it was in my power to correct, yes, I was going to have a torrid time telling my parents about it one day, yes, wasn't it dreadful that there had been a cottage industry in Ireland in exporting the illegitimate to suburban English homes? But, just like everyone else, I was tired of being a floating voter; I just wanted to be plugged in somewhere, to know about a place where, if all had gone well, I truly belonged.

My visit to the adoption society had given me a lot of information, including one massive clue. Instead of being Paul Arnott, 11.11.61, I was now Rory Brennan, 11.11.61. The former was the name I had always had and would never disown, but it was a name that opened no doors. Rory

Brennan had a place on the shelves with the real people, and I could hardly wait to get back to St Catherine's House to find him.

The Indian summer broke, but for the time being my involvement with the real India continued. I was setting up a programme I was to make in November about the London Film Festival for Doordashan, the Indian state broadcaster. This involved dealing with two of the worst bureaucracies on Earth, the Indian government and the British Film Institute. When I eventually had time to get to St Catherine's, which seemed the model of enlightened governance by comparison, it was on a cold, rainy October afternoon about ten minutes before the building was due to close.

Coming out of the Aldwych rain into the dull interior of the Office of Population Censuses and Surveys, the General Register Office, and preparing deliberately to unveil a decades-old secret, I felt like a character from a Graham Greene novel. Being able to go, not to the adoptive birth register, with its informational dead ends, but to the ordinary, widescreen, unstigmatised birth records was like escaping from the old Soviet bloc to the lands of milk and honey in the West. I took the massive register for the quarter of my birth date down off the shelf and looked for my new old name, Rory Brennan. Born 11 November 1961. A cross-reference number for my original birth certificate, up to a counter to fill in an application form, and back into the rain with the promise that it would be posted on to me.

A few days later the duplicate of my original birth certificate arrived, and its generous proportions did not disappoint. The appearance of the word 'Adopted' entered by the registrar at the end seemed truly shocking on what otherwise was the document everyone else took for granted, a grim word like 'Amputated' or 'Stillborn'. It was a chill reminder that this was not a matter to be taken lightly. The fact that my own name, Paul Arnott, appeared nowhere on the certificate reinforced the impression that this was the birth certificate of someone who could have led an altogether different life if only the entry of that word 'Adopted' had been avoided.

Just as at the adoption society, there was also a farcical element about this. When I discovered that I was of Irish origin it hadn't been great luck of the draw for my quest to learn that my natural father's name was Brennan, which is up there with Kelly and Walsh in the Irish phone directory. What the certificate could give me, perhaps crucially, was my mother's maiden name. And there it was, column five, first entry, next to her Christian name, Ann. Ann Jones.

2

A False Start

A GLITTERING pair of contemporary myths are currently at large, relating to the final enlightenment that will come to us courtesy of the age of information via the twin tracks of genetics and the Internet. Almost every day I dash across a room to switch off yet another radio discussion about the first of these myths – the effect on our humanity of the mapping of the human genome. Lacking any other novel idea, this is the new frontier for many intellectuals, whose early predictions for how we will at last meet the ghost in the machine seem to be the height of deterministic hyperbole. The discovery of genetic predeterminants in the pathology of painful diseases undoubtedly will represent a breakthrough in the art of medicine, but these mutant genes can only be discovered precisely because we already know that, unfortunately, there is such a medical problem as cancer of the breast. The disease and the gene match;

in seeking to match them we know exactly what we are looking for.

But when it comes to finding genetic determinants for anything to do with the human psyche, it is and will remain a fool's errand. Scarcely a single one of us can agree, for example, on what intelligence is, on the purpose of altruism, who or what is the god-shaped hole within, how we can be happy, whether man and woman should mate for life or just for Christmas. If we don't know what we're looking for in the pseudo-science of the mind, then there certainly isn't a double helix for it. What we can be sure of, in a continuation of the human tragicomedy of the less well placed swallowing the profitable theories of the great and the good, is that someone is about to claim that they will soon have a genetic map of the human psyche. And we can be just as sure that there will be charlatans and politicians who will attempt to gain power by the misuse of this map. The tragedy of this will be that, like so many other manmade maps over the centuries, it will be a lie and a big one at that.

I first learned to resist the big genetic idea in the field of human intelligence as an occasionally diligent student of psychology twenty years ago, when confronted with what seemed already then to be the shrivelled chestnut of the nature versus nurture debate in human intelligence. Through the study of separated twins Sir Cyril Burt had shown that intelligence was indeed inherited beyond any doubt – the fly in the ointment here being that he had made up all his research and the twins had not been separated at all. In fact, they didn't exist. All these chaps were fun to read, but like Freud himself they formed classic cases of producing a flattering confirmation of the hypothesis you had in the first place.

In the case of most of those working in the field of intelligence, all too often a thinly veiled eugenicist strain tried to answer two questions. Why are common people so terribly thick? And why am I, Professor Sparkle, so fabulously intelligent? The answer, as any parent knows, is Education. Ah, but what kind should we give them? The self-evident answer here is lots of it, in small classes, with nice teachers, some fun, a field and a strong ethos. And unless a child is unfortunate enough to have a genuine medical disability or a mild functional problem like dyslexia, that's all you need to know to give a child a chance to move away from any social or emotional disadvantage of its lot in life.

But if the reawakening of genetic determinism was a fool's errand then I'd come to believe the fool's gold to be that second mythic entity, the Internet search engine. Again, I reasoned, what your eyes will read through the screen can only ever be a product of the information that has been put on the Net in the first place. My early online forays into adoption confirmed my prejudice. Crouched over my keyboard I entered the word 'Adoption' into my search engine and pressed the return key. What wealth of understanding, what new connections of the mind would be yielded to me? Seconds later came my answer.

Thousands upon thousands of results of my search had been located. At last, in cyberspace, would I find a brotherhood of the adopted?

I clicked tensely on the first result of my search. What wisdom would be mine? Words in a primal font surged on to my screen. 'Adopt a Rhino at Whipsnade Zoo'. And that wasn't all. There were dogs, cats, tigers, elephants all crying out for adoption in the search results listed below, in hundreds of links uploaded by zoos and cat fanciers around the world. The nearest thing to me was 'Adopt a London Chimpanzee'. Very well, I reasoned, man is but one of the creatures on God's earth. Let's go down a few pages. Ah, here at last was Man: 'The Adoption of the Ordnance Survey Map as the mapping template for Durham Council'. What? Where was I? Down again: 'The Adoption of the State Sewage Plan by the Milwaukee Legislative Assembly'.

Just as I'd thought, I said to the empty office, it's just a Tower of Babel. I brewed myself a mug of Ceylon tea, returned to my desk and scrolled down page by page until at last this journey into absurdity took a sharp turn into sheer pathos. Here was the first item I had ever located on the Internet that related to the adoption of a human child. It was headed, in pink, 'A Mother's Search'.

On 14th April 1964 I gave birth to a boy at St Mary's Hospital, Manchester, England. I called him Simon. Through what was at the time no fault of mine, through events and circumstances beyond my control, I was forced to have him adopted. I have tried through all the After Adoption Agencies but because of the laws of England the information I can obtain is little or non-existent. He was adopted by a couple who lived in the Birkenhead area of the Wirral, England called John and Maureen – they had him christened Andrew. The adoption was made legal on 15th October 1964. John was born in 1930 and was in the Merchant Navy. Maureen was born in 1934 and worked as a shop assistant. I understand that they also adopted another boy in 1961, Mark. Andrew, as he has been known for the majority of his life, I understand may now be living abroad from England, with his wife and child. I have found out Andrew and his family may have emigrated while he was young, the country I do not know.

Whatever you can tell me would be gratefully received and treated in the strictest of confidence. I would like to thank all the people who have sent me messages of goodwill and encouragement, and for the people also searching for loved ones my sincere good wishes that one day you will find what you desire.

By the time I had read this woman's appeal my dry eyes, which had crinkled with pompous amusement at the idea of the Whipsnade rhino, were filled with reluctant tears. For here, in her short summary of her search, this woman's dilemma expressed in microcosm that of many millions of others. The child she'd borne, given up, never forgotten, always loved, was a child she now had no rights in law to find. I clicked a little further into this single website, one of the thousands, and there were other searchers with similar tales, from West Virginia, Blackpool, Ontario, the United Arab Emirates, Sussex. On and on the tales, the quests ran, and without exception they prompted further tears. They were, I knew, tears of recognition. There was no need to resort to the classics to find universal stories of lost children; at the end of the twentieth century they were just a click away. And they were tears, I suppose, of validation, for in the account of this woman looking for Simon was precisely the mindset that I had already attributed to the mother I had never met.

Above all, perhaps, my tears were of both anger and disappointment. How had the human race allowed its women to find themselves in the position where they had to give up the child they had made, and then know nothing, not a jot of detail, of what became of it? How did we allow these women's distress to go so ignored that they had to resort to pleas for help from complete strangers via a technological development that had thus far proved itself mainly as a place where a generation of men growing hair on the palms of their hands may interact with a fiery hell of hard-core pornography?

Adoption has a history. Many of the academic studies of the subject are as dry as a bone, but one of the experts has summarised its beginning and its end with a rare wit:

The first recorded adoption in Western tradition is that of Moses, a transcultural and possibly transracial adoption in which the infant of a subjugated parent was adopted by a woman of the ruling class, possibly a single parent. No agency was involved, with the birth family watching over the child until he was found. Secrecy was partially preserved in the adoption with the identity of the birth parent being concealed from the adopting parent. The motive of the adopting parent was compassion, the motive of the birth parent the need to find a home for her child. Thus in many ways this first recorded adoption catches elements of adoptions through time.[*]

Any history of adoption usually kicks off thus with Moses, confidently sprinting on through time to describe how a Roman with no heir would adopt a son for the continuation of his name and the good of his large estate groaning with grapes and olives. Julius Caesar adopted Octavius, who became Caesar Augustus, which does not please me. Mark Antony, or Shakespeare's version of him, was always my man, and I'd always thought Octavius to be the epitome of cold calculation and a total shit.

Then, as with all history, the adoption account seems to enter a Dark Age. Academics sometimes try to paper this

[*] John Triselotis, Joan Shirema, Marion Hundleby, *Adoption: Theory, Policy and Practice,* Cassell, 1997.

over by taking us to the South Pacific islands, where adoption is said always to have been common and where the child and birth mother are said not to have had to relinquish contact with each other. Or on to the Hindu Law of Manu, which allowed for adoption, or to the Koran, which very specifically didn't. Historians are then relieved to return from the ethnic fringe when they reach the end of the Middle Ages. Here both the Catholic Church and the reformed churches in Europe were not prepared to dilute the sanctity of marriage as the only legal union for procreation and so refused to recognise adoption as a legitimate procedure for caring for what they were happy to condemn as nature's offcut, the illegitimate. Adoption was off the menu.

There is a consensus, though, on the later effects of the Industrial Revolution and the new supremacy of the city over the countryside as the home of the majority of the population. Cities, unlike villages, were anonymous, taboos broke down, alcohol was drunk, sex was had and the result was regiments of orphans across Europe and the Eastern Seaboard of the United States. Orphanages were opened and unwed mothers had to relinquish their children to baby-farming houses where they were sometimes fed a mixture of laudanum, lime, cornflour, water, milk and washing powder. Needless to say many of these babies then died, but the baby-farmers had it both ways. A dead baby paid out in insurance; a live one could be sold to the highest bidder.

Fortunately for the orphans, however, on both sides of the Atlantic Dickensian villains had their match in well-intentioned social reformers. Thomas Coram used the royalties from Handel's *Messiah* to rescue children from the street and take them into his foundlings' hospital. As a nine-year-old I sang in *The Messiah* myself and was left with one of those great misunderstandings of the childhood imagination. One of the treble's lines was 'For the Lord God Omni-potent reigneth', the dash between *omni* and *potent* breaking a long word to fit with the score. I was doing my A-levels before I realised that there was no god called Omni, and neither did he reign in a particularly potent fashion.

Developments in America in the mid-nineteenth century began to formalise the concept and law of adoption for the first time in history. The catalyst was the movement, begun by Charles Loring Brace and his New York-based Children's Aid Society in 1856, that was known as 'placing out', the young beneficiaries of which came to be known as Orphan Train Riders. Imagine for a moment a classic railroad train like the one Casey Jones used to ride, only this train was filled with hundreds of well-scrubbed children from the tenement slums of Brooklyn. It's a train that would head out into the Mid-West of America, where large farming families needed extra hands and were prepared to take in and eventually adopt a 'stranger of the blood'. At each station the children dismounted and were 'put up' for adoption in a straightforward beauty parade. By the time the train reached the end of the line it was hoped that there would be no child left on board.

It was an extraordinary passage in American history, with 200,000 children known to have been adopted in this way until the 1920s, when social criticism brought the practice to an end, but not before this wholesale placement of slum children had mirrored the development of the American West:

In 1850 there were 9,021 miles of track in the United States; by 1875 there were 74,096; and by the end of the century the number had increased to 192,556 miles, with 1,224 operating railways. Placement of the eastern poor corresponded directly to expanding the rail service. First limited to the eastern states with rail connections to metropolitan centers, placing out was extended in the mid 1850s to states of the old Northwest Territory with their growing miles of rails. When railroad companies began to build west of the Mississippi after the Civil War these regions drew the attention of placing-out institutions. Increased miles of track moving ever west, south and southwest allowed the transport of the eastern poor farther along the line, and railroad hubs such as Chicago, St Louis and Kansas City became the staging grounds from which the placed out, brought that far, could be sent to final destinations. As one man, seventy-two years after his placing-out experience, recalled: 'We boarded the . . . train somewhere close to New York City (in 1915). The train had four coaches with about

40 orphans each. In St Louis, Missouri, the train divided and the coaches went to four different states, Kansas, Missouri, Oklahoma, and Arkansas. My coach went to Berryville, Ark.'*

Today the memory of these children is kept alive by a voluntary organisation called the Orphan Train Heritage Society of America, based in Springdale, Arizona. In a nation where a clear sense of one's roots is central to a clear sense of one's identity, it has been possible for the descendants of these children to claim an extra helping of historical background, their forebears having been probably the most innocent of the colonisers of the West. And as an organisation it is almost the quintessence of what America likes to think about itself – rooted, interested, positive and enthusiastic. If its happiness with itself represented a true snapshot of the state of mind of those Americans who had been adopted and their offspring, that would be a marvellous thing.

Sadly, it can be argued that another American organisation is nearer to the true heart of the dilemmas of adoption. Its name: Bastard Nation, a potent adoptee rights lobby born in 1996. It was the very success of the Orphan Trains that led indirectly to its foundation. As the placing-out movement grew, it was eventually criticised for not following up

* Marilyn Irvin Holt, *The Orphan Trains – Placing Out in America*. University of Nebraska Press, 1992.

on the success or failure of placements nor for taking care to place children with new parents of like religion, which resulted in America leading the way in adoption legislation. The positive side of this during the last century is that new statutes on both sides of the Atlantic would protect children like me from exploitation and placement with lunatics. The negative side was that the formalisation of the process of adoption would eventually lead to the shrouding of an adoption in official secrecy, which would eventually place individuals like myself in a quite impossible position.

The problem arose mainly in the period just after the First World War, which created hundreds of thousands of orphans in England and America, and during the Great Depression, which created thousands more. The demand for children for well-off middle-class homes was rising, and the supply was booming, but as most adoptions were privately arranged or organised by adoption societies that were not subject to any central registration, there was widespread concern that the state must act to prevent malpractice. The net result, however, was the creation of an entirely accidental twist in the adoption experience of people such as myself. Probably the best academic study of this subject is by the American writer E. Wayne Carp:

> The origins for the inclusion of confidentiality clauses in state legislation had little to do with preventing adult adoptees and adoptive parents from viewing

their adoption records; they were never the initial target of the legislation. The wording of the statutes, contemporary statements from state legislators, and existent commentary by social workers indicate that the laws' original purpose was to keep the *public* from viewing the records, not those who had a personal stake in the adoption proceeding. The Children's Code of Wisconsin, for example, justified the confidentiality clause of its 1929 revision of the adoption statute on the basis that 'curious and unscrupulous persons formerly might secure and disclose much information with regard to illegitimacy and other circumstance connected with adoption matters.' Likewise, California legislators successfully introduced a bill to place adoption records in a 'secret file' because of several cases 'where unscrupulous persons have obtained access to the adoption records and blackmailed the adopted parents by threatening to tell the child it was adopted.'*

What Carp has demonstrated is that it was never the intention to prevent adopted children from one day finding out who their birth parents were, but to prevent nosy parkers from stirring up trouble by brandishing the word 'illegitimate' while these children were growing up. But

---

* E. Wayne Carp, *Family Matters – Secrecy and Disclosure in the History of Adoption*. Harvard University Press, 1998.

what has evolved in the United States over the last fifty years is a mess. Until recently, only two states, Alaska and Kansas, allowed adoptees at the age of eighteen to have unconditional access to their birth records. More typically, Montana has open records for those adopted before 1967, but you need a court order to open records for adoptions between 1967 and 1997. For adoptions since 1997 an adoptee can obtain records at the age of eighteen, but the birth parent has a right to veto this.

Bastard Nation had its genesis in an American adoption-related website, and soon splintered off to become an independent, campaigning entity. It came out punching, and in November 1998 it led a successful referendum campaign in Oregon to pass Measure 58, which would make it the first state to open unconditionally the previously sealed records of adult adoptees. The validity of this reform was challenged through the Oregon Supreme Court right up until the summer of 2000, until finally the US Supreme Court denied a motion to stay the measure. It was a bloody campaign, with regiments of birth mothers and adoptees fighting their opposing corners, and it will take dozens more such fights for the US as a whole to reform. However, it was a brave and ruthless beginning for this devastating lobbying force, which draws its power from the degree of free speech and exchange of information – from rallying dates to true-life tales – made possible by the Internet.

What seems to have made the blood of Bastard Nation boil is that the whole process of secrecy in adoption has become, tragically, a politicised issue. There are many groups in America who regard the soaring number of abortions as an affront to God, and they will do anything to support adoption as an alternative. Far from believing that now is the time to open all records, to bring an end to the age of secrets and lies, they want adoption records to be sealed for a mandatory ninety-nine years. They believe that it is in the best interest of the child and of the adoptive parents for the child to be able to start with a *tabula rasa* and for adoption to be an absolute. It will come as no surprise that this movement, who support the draft Uniform Adoption Act, is known to be mainly from the religious right under the banner of the National Council for Adoption.

This grouping is on a collision course with Bastard Nation and there seems no room for compromise. Bastard Nation is a classic 'rights' organisation that believes that all adoptees should have the freedom to choose whether they trace their birth parents or not. They believe in the right for all people to have access to their original birth record 'unaltered and free from falsification', and the fact that someone is adopted should not prevent them exercising this right. What makes them such a thorn in the whole industry of adoption, from social workers to politicians, is that they are not interested in the middle ground:

Bastard Nation does not support mandated mutual consent registries or intermediary systems in place of fully open records, nor any other system that is less than access on demand to the adult adoptee, without compromise and without qualification.

This refusal in one of their stated tenets to compromise, particularly to allow the involvement of an intermediary, seems at first sight unduly radical and brazenly insensitive. But these people live in a country whose constitution is all about rights. They argue that each person has a right to his own history and identity, and that since they are just as competent to manage their affairs as non-adoptees they should be able to proceed without the enforced supervision of the state. And they simply don't like social workers, whose intermediary role gives enormous and often unaccountable power and discretion in assessing the 'suitability' and 'maturity' of an adoptee's application for their original birth records. In a field abundant with secrets and lies it sticks in the throat of Bastard Nation to have to pay social workers for the privilege of what they fear will be another pile of secrets and lies when someone rejects their application without telling them why.

I know what they mean. Perhaps being adopted in the first place does make one prone to suspicion of authority. The only winners in all this are the TV shows. It's great daytime television. In the left corner is a thirty-five-year-old adoptee with a serious medical condition who needs to locate her family for a bone marrow transplant and does not have the unhindered right to find Mom. In the right corner, in an unlit part of the studio, is Barbara, forty-five, who was raped as a nineteen-year-old and had the child of that encounter adopted. She's now a mother of three and the beloved wife of a man she had never told about either the rape or the adoption. The last thing she wants is a twenty-six-year-old cuckoo in her settled life.

As with most journalism, the most vivid colour is located where there is a contrast of extremes. Most adoption cases are far more prosaic – no disease, no rape, just a cock-up. But when journalists and politicians and churchmen become involved, the whole issue acquires a series of ugly kinks. In a way I am grateful both to the subject of adoption and to American television. I have worked in television in London myself, all pretty blameless stuff about the arts. (Lord Reith would have lost no sleep, anyway.) But the combination of studying adoption, having a semi-professional incontinent finger on the TV blipper and being awoken for the thousandth time by one of my children in the middle of the night meant that I was witness to the worst piece of television ever made:

'All right. Tonight on Jerry Springer [who else?] we're looking at people who are trying to find lost loved ones. Now Clare [sitting alone on stage] was forced to give her children up for adoption twenty years ago. It's a decision she's had to live with, maybe one she's learned to regret [Camera 2 Big Close Up on moist-eyed Clare. Jerry turns to Camera 4, sotto voce]. But what Clare doesn't know is that we've found those *two children* [Backstage Camera on the two children in their early twenties] *and that tonight we're going to reunite them right here.* [Chorus of "Jerry, Jerry".]'

I admit that it was 2.30 a.m. and I was watching this masterpiece just after putting a vomit-covered sheet into the washing machine. I thought to myself that this couldn't be genuine. I mean, surely there was some broadcasting regulation to prevent this. Clare must know. Doesn't she? But there was no stopping Jerry. He opened Clare up entirely, and she was exposed as unbelievably sad, someone who seemed to define vulnerability. Christ, I thought, this isn't a set-up. She really doesn't know.

'*So, Clare, the thing you'd really like is just to hear from your two birth children, maybe talk, one day meet.* [Clare nods, clearly hoping that someone out there will have made a connection with her pleas.] *Well, Clare, you don't have to wait anymore, because we've found them.* [Studio in stony silence, like moment before the kill at a bullfight. Clare looks shocked, can't find words.] *And they're here, and what they want more than anything is to meet you.* [Stage left enter the two children. Clare looks as if she has been hit by a truck. They run towards each other. They all embrace. More "Jerry, Jerry". Then Jerry makes them sit down. The problem is that Clare is now shaking with shock. Women sometimes do this after giving birth, a terrifying spasm of release. Clare's doing it for Jerry.]'

How angry was I after seeing this? This was defile-a-soul TV. Clare shouldn't have had to be there, her life a one-minute wonder, living soap. Surely the American constitution allows for dignity to go with life, liberty and the pursuit of happiness. And if the people from Bastard Nation prevailed, Jerry would never be able to cash this particular cheque again. Maybe they were right.

On Wednesday 12 November 1975 my parents and over half a million others in England and Wales were reluctantly cast in a leading role in an entirely new adoption myth. For centuries before that day, the prevailing myth of adoption had been that of Oedipus. (Curiously, birth records are still shut in Greece and Bastard Nation are affiliated to an adoption rights organisation in Athens.) The main thing to beware of, if you were adopted, was unwittingly ending up in bed with your natural mother/father/sister/brother. It was mainly a matter of not attempting to seduce those who looked precisely like you, but the consequences were generally agreed to involve termination with extreme prejudice. You were more than likely to make tempting subject matter for anyone from Sophocles to Jeffrey Archer.

In 1975 the law changed so that adopted children, on reaching the age of eighteen and after counselling, could obtain access to their original birth certificates. Now, the possibility was not that you might sleep with your mother (not accidentally anyway), but that you were empowered as an adopted child both to return to haunt the lives of those who had conceived you while simultaneously destroying the illusions of those who had raised you, fed you and in all probability loved you as strongly as if you had been made from their own flesh and blood.

You can see that this is a tricky one. The adopted child, taking a very English, reserved, muted tack, which is in effect identical to that of Bastard Nation, decides to trace and to exercise what is his moral and legal right. Who has the most to lose if that child does trace? Not the adoptee, who has an adventure ahead, at the end of which can only be knowledge, even if it is a horrible discovery. Not the birth parent, who at worst is having their mind put at rest (and if they don't care, then it doesn't matter anyway) and at best is having their life reanimated by their lost child, usually a first-born. No, the party with the most to lose is the adoptive parents.

Clearly it is in the best interest of the adoptive parents to take the hit of a few days of hurt feelings and to support the adoptee (from a distance) as he searches. And this doesn't seem such a high price to pay for the part that child has played in their lives. It's a back tax, but it's not one they cannot afford. But people do not always do what is in their own best interests, and it is not unknown for adoptive parents being told of their child's search to go for a standard 'you ungrateful little bastard' line. It is for fear of this that many adopted children do not trace, or leave it until both adoptive parents are dead. The difficulty with this is that the adopted child could easily be in his fifties by the time this happens, with a trail grown even colder and, quite possibly, a natural mother's heart bearing a needless extra two decades of grieving for her lost child.

Nevertheless this is the deal that my parents' generation were sold and it would be hard-hearted not to sympathise with them. In 1961, when I was adopted, I became my parents' and my parents' alone. Fourteen years later the goalposts were moved, and there are still many adoptive parents who consider this unfair. The problem is that life is full of deals that turn out not to be at all what we are sold. I was told an endowment policy would pay off my mortgage. That's a laugh. I was told that my 1987 personal computer would run for fifty years. Well, it's not actually rusty, but it is so absolutely millennium-non-compliant that I plan to keep it in the cellar to show my grandchildren. A child is not a mortgage or a white good. Sadly, some human hearts run on bloody instinct, not on the thin gases of the greater good.

I used to think this was of little real significance, but now I know it is the most significant thing in the world. We all have a first memory, don't we? At a fishmonger's, in a car that overheats, falling over on a beach, the instant when your conscious mind awakened.

My memory starts twice. My first memory is having a bath in a sink in a hotel room in Tenby at the age of two, looking out of the window to the beach changing huts below. Your first memory might be similar, or it might be hideous, like receiving a beating or seeing something dead in the road.

My *second* first memory is one you will not have if, like my children, you have been or are being raised by the people who conceived and gave birth to you. It is the Bromley afternoon when Mr and Mrs Arnott plucked up their courage and delivered the following news. 'Paul,' my mother began, 'we have something to tell you. You know that Daddy and I love you very much? Well, we were not your first Mummy and Daddy. Your real Mummy and Daddy couldn't keep you, and so they had to have you "adopted". And so they gave you to some people who gave you to us. And now you are ours.' This, as you might imagine, was big news, especially for a three-year-old. Following the recommended script my parents went on, 'What's wonderful is that you are extra special because we chose to have you – you were chosen. You are a special child.'

Now, as I understand it from many of the legion of adopted illegitimates walking our land, this issue of special-ness can be taken two ways. You believe it, or you don't. You either cleave to the adoptive family, eternally grateful and loving, a joy to all, or, if you are the bastard of the ungrateful variety, as I have been called, you don't.

My real first memory, therefore, royal and triumphant in my seaside sink, is pastoral, pleasing. My second first memory was like the moment when NASA pushed the igni-tion button to blast Apollo Nine to the moon. It was the moment at which my blood was catalysed so that it would be sufficient to power my spirit until it reached a planet where I might attain the big (but apparently tricky) three – to fall in love, to marry, and to have a child myself – and in so doing put things right.

Brutally, grateful as I was to my parents, my immediate, permanent and deep reading of their tale was that some nameless twerp had been stupid enough to, in effect, mislay me. Further, my poor parents, who had their own reasons, unimaginable to me, had simply taken me in.

This didn't feel special. It felt like a cock-up. But, if I could just have enough zest in my blood to complete the trajectory from childhood via education to adulthood and independence, I could restart the whole misbegotten exercise of reproduction, be sure not to mislay my own offspring, and thus ensure that the world would once again run even, upon even ground.

For my parents the act of creating this second first memory must have been like holding a baby while the doctor jabs its first inoculations through its unpierced skin. But, unlike that first injection, it was also a moment when my parents were unknowingly exposing themselves to something they had not conceived they would ever have to face. For, once this painful injection of truth had been given, everything was then meant to be all right, over. In 1961, when a natural mother gave her baby to be adopted the understanding on both her part and that of the adopting parents was that this was an irreversible cauterisation.

The mother had no residual rights in relation to the child, and the child would self-evidently never have access to that most potent of documents – its original birth certificate.

This is peculiar stuff – first, two first memories, now two birth certificates. And in my case, two birth certificates with two completely different names. I spent thirty-three years as Paul Arnott, only to discover that in another part of the world a married couple were wondering what on earth had happened to one Rory Brennan. Rory, the first-born son who, if they hadn't lived in a time of all powerful priests and supine congregations, would have been raised by them but who instead, because he was conceived illegitimately three months before they were married, got left behind.

But I did not spend my childhood weeping in my sleep. In my conscious mind, and in the fiercely self-protective way that children have, from 1964 to about 1979 I didn't give the fact of being adopted a moment's thought. Some part of the engine was shut off, although it was not jettisoned.

I have one single adoption memory from that period, one rock in a deep pool. It was 1967. I was six, and it was a Sunday morning in spring. My father reversed the Morris Oxford out of the garage, and drove us cross-suburb from Bromley Common to West Clandon in north Surrey. The friends of my parents we were to visit for lunch were Frank and Doreen. That late Sunday morning was spent in their attic, where Frank had built for his children Susan and Stephen (and himself, I suspected) one of those major model railway set-ups, where branch line trains scoot around a plywood structure in the centre of which is a hole. You could crawl to the hole, stand up at the middle of this world, and control the system from a sequence of amply-knobbed boxes. I was mildly interested in all this, but was glad when the call came to go down to Sunday lunch. Little worlds were weird worlds for me, since subconsciously I was always seeking signals from the planet of certain universal rules of normality, rather than of grown men playing with train sets.

I bounced downstairs and into the dining room, where we sat at the polished table and began to eat our Sunday lunch. There was a silence. My father, mother, brother, Frank, Susan, and Stephen were all chewing. I wasn't. I was gazing at Doreen. She was slim, pretty, with bright blue eyes, thick, wavy, dark hair, and a strong, potentially pointed nose. Thinking of myself as a little man I ignored Frank's right to choose the first topic of conversation. I put my knife and fork down, looked Doreen straight in the eye, and said, 'You look just like my real mother.'

I would have caused less embarrassment if I had simply removed my trousers and poohed in the fruit bowl. But the fact remained – this woman looked precisely like the picture I had in my head of the woman who was my real mother, a picture that until that moment I did not know was in my head at all.

But what was most potent about this outburst, apart from the total humiliation it visited on my parents as Frank and Doreen were forced to put aside the sprouts and explain to their children the basics of adoption, is that when I received the first photograph of my natural mother, twenty-seven years later, a picture taken in the late sixties, she looked exactly like Doreen Butcher. To date I am unable to explain how I knew what my real mother looked like, but at the age of six know it I did.

But then, after 1967, the trail went cold.

I quickly noticed that to be different at school was to be liable to merciless mocking. Fortunately, apart from the big head (which was the biggest clue to my later destiny) I had nothing obviously awry for the mockers to mock. Even though my four closest friends today are people I have known from the age of ten or before, the last thing I wanted to do was admit that I was not entirely the picture of normality they had chosen as their friend.

Thus the first person on the planet I told about the fact of my adoption was my first girlfriend, Christina, in 1979. It seemed to me that since she was prepared to visit the family doctor, a man who acted opposite her mother in the St Luke's Players, and request a Dutch cap and two tubes of spermicide, I owed her the truth and nothing but the truth. I now realise I was very lucky that it was Christina I told. It may be that some devious, adolescent, adopted boys use their condition as some kind of sob story to lure romantically minded girls to bed. The very thought would have appalled me, and fortunately Christina privately

judged that I was not ready to explore the resonances of
my confession, and was careful to give the impression that
this new information was of no more significance to her
than knowing my blood group. Having told her, I began
gradually to tell my friends, all of whom reacted with
similar equanimity.

This previously repressed part of my life was now beginning to seep from its tank, and from 1979 onwards I began
slowly to evolve the makings of idle thought. Adopted
people, apparently, come up with some choice hypotheses
of who their real parents might be – the Duke of Edinburgh
seems to figure, mysteriously, in many such speculations.
As an ultra-optimistic pessimist I mainly settled for the
idea of an East End, heroin-addicted mother who died in
labour. That way I wasn't missing anything.

These days the mirror tells me that if I actually resemble
anyone famous it's Elvis just before he limped to the loo
that lonesome, last time. (With four children, I haven't
slept or exercised properly since 1990.) But for three years
in the early eighties, just before I looked like Rodney
Bewes, it was said that I looked like Paul McCartney.
Once, I was crossing a bridge over the River Exe and a
nine year old thought I was the bloke out of the 'Ebony
and Ivory' video with Michael Jackson, and could he have
my autograph? As a consequence of this encounter, I
nipped to the library and worked out that even though
McCartney would have been very young, he could indeed
have impregnated the heroin addict after some early

concert, when they were still called The Quarrymen, and I could be the result. Thought does not come much more idle than this.

However, my inexplicable, impossible vision of my mother in 1967 would slip to the surface of my mind, year after year, at the oddest moments. Sadly, those I saw most of, my mum and dad, were the last people I could talk to about it. This seems to me one of the terrible flaws of the era of total adoption where all birth roots were severed – unless the child was raised by a Nobel-prize-winning psychotherapist, this landmine of identity remained buried and undefused.

Yet the childhood memories I have of my parents and my upbringing are otherwise full of pleasure – a blue E-type Jaguar pedal car I adored, blue toy binoculars and the funicular railway at Babbacombe beach, being given my first Coca-Cola on a journey with my dad when I'd been car-sick – standard-issue, fond, secure memories of obviously being loved and, I think, loving in return. We talked about adoption twice, and both times I said I had no interest in tracing my birth parents. The first time they asked me was when I was doing my A-levels, and the second was just before I married. With hindsight, these were both moments of transition for my mum and dad as much as me, and it was they who raised the subject. Whilst they were probably worrying about these rites of passage, I can honestly say that the last thing on my mind during my A-levels, or just before my wedding, was creating any additional complications by a hunt for missing persons. My parents had probably picked two of the least appropriate moments to ask, and I swatted the question away with zero consideration and a pat negative.

Now, here I was, ten years later, with my original birth certificate. Often, the truth in matters of the heart is utterly prosaic, and the truth was, I did not want to involve my parents in my adoption quest at this stage – in exactly the same way that I didn't want to involve them in my sex life, my tax affairs, my bowel movements, or my marriage. I hadn't lived at home for fifteen years and I was dependent upon them for nothing. When the time came to tell them, I would do it, but my every instinct was screaming that that time was not now.

3

Here Comes the Flood

I NOW had symptoms similar to the sickness of unrequited love. I knew a little, I had my birth certificate, I was processing very slowly and very dimly the implications of Irishness (and resisting their significance) but I was as far from a tangible result now as I had ever been. All sorts of homespun remarks – a little knowledge is a dangerous thing, for example – acquired a significance well beyond their worth. And everywhere I looked, like wraiths rising from the earth, I was aware for the first time of the profound importance to others of their parental roots.

In our short road there were Turks and Greeks (all Cypriot in origin but getting on fine in the UK), Germans, Sri Lankans, Scots, Jamaicans, Tamils, English. Over the last few hundred years many of these groups had warred with, exploited or betrayed the other, yet in our road they got along just fine. I was very confused as to whether it was better, as in the song, to consign everyone to a great big melting pot and 'make coffee-coloured people by the score', or whether our street showed that so long as ethnic diversity is allowed to exist in a tolerant society then differences of identity should be a matter of pride.

Lydia does not allow me to bring the *Sun* into the house. Why I still read it is a complex matter with which she has no patience, as she considers it the house journal of the sexist moron. My defence – that since 1979 it had been the best way to find out what black propaganda the Conservative government were planning next – was given short shrift. Therefore I had got used, on occasion, to slipping it inside my *Guardian*, reading it at the speed of light and shoving it into the dustbin before I was caught. Pathetic, isn't it? Now, inside the *Sun* inside the *Guardian* I was smuggling the *Irish News* or *Irish World*, two weekly papers published in the UK. It was a time of headlines about peace talks, priests fathering children and the identification of the Irish as a relatively impoverished 'ethnic minority'. It was also a time of Irish soccer triumphs (relative to England), the extraordinary growth in the transformation of dull English locals into Irish-themed pubs, and the sanctification of Ireland's first woman president, Mary Robinson.

The sections of these papers that most interested me were the photographic snaps, arrayed in centre-page spreads, of the Coventry Galway Society or the Birmingham Irish Businessmen's Guild Annual Dinner.

For the first time ever I was seeing pictures of groups of people who looked like I do in photographs. For even with the sharpest lens and the best film stock I always look out of focus, sort of fat-faced, smiling a smile that seems inebriated even though it is not, with my best feature, the blue eyes, squished into red-pupilled slits. And here they were, hundreds of them, medium height, medium build, out of focus. Was I one of *them*?

This wasn't an identity crisis, far from it. It was a combination of my conscious and unconscious minds boning up on the subject of Irishness in a situation where I knew and appreciated French life and culture much more.

My meanderings were almost immediately thrown into sharp relief when my working life led me to engage with people for whom national and ethnic identity were significant on, it seemed to me, an infinitely more momentous scale.

By now it was mid-autumn and I was producing and directing the programme from the London Film Festival, with Derek Malcolm, the experienced and respected film critic of the *Guardian*, as presenter. I'd worked with Derek at various film festivals from Cannes to Bangalore, but suddenly I was paying attention to the stories of his past – an Etonian, not very tall, a Scot with a fair amount of family tragedy, once a jockey, then a racing correspondent, a cricket correspondent and finally a film critic, indeed for many of the international film community *the* critic. As a former director of the London Film Festival he had been

instrumental in making it what it was – non-competitive,
thoroughly international, and while not actually allergic to
Hollywood then at least sceptical about its wares.

For the programme we interviewed some of the best-
regarded directors and producers from around the world,
and what they all had in common was that none of them
came from Bromley, Kent, and all of their work was
profoundly bound up with their own sense of personal
identity. There was Ismail Merchant of Merchant Ivory,
producers of what were perceived in the United Kingdom
as classics of novel adaptation, the epitome of Englishness.
Yet here he sat, Asian, gay, producing an American director, living here, there and everywhere, and when the money
ran out on set still with the trick that he would cook a huge
meal, personally, for the cast and crew. He was promoting
The Remains of the Day with Anthony Hopkins as a butler
giving the definitive account of the English capacity for the
repression of love for the sake of duty.

Merchant was also promoting his own debut as a director, *In Custody*, with the supreme Indian actor Shashi
Kapoor as a broken-hearted aging poet. And Merchant had
made the brave decision that he would shoot the film in
Urdu, one of the many Indian dialects, and not one that
had previously travelled well across the world. Not for the
first time I thought that the United Kingdom and the
Republic of Ireland's quarrels with each other were feeble,
over-inflated and parochial compared to the kind of
mammoth balancing act that a billion Indians were

performing every day in their sheer diversity. I was also reminded that for many artists across the world they have to leave their country of origin to achieve anything of any worth.

The Chinese director, Chen Kaige, was at the festival for *Farewell My Concubine*, which had won the Palme d'Or at Cannes earlier in the year. After our interview with him at the last night party I was probably far too effusive in my thanks, but I was deeply grateful for the context in which he put my own quandaries. Chen had dedicated the film to his father. In the West we are spoiled by this dedication business, when Oscar winners thank their pedicurist for making them a whole person and so on. Chen, however, was speaking with devastating honesty: 'My life is like the film. My life was all about the Cultural Revolution and what happened to me in it. Like in the film, I denounced my own father in front of the public. You know, he was a film-maker too. But at the moment I denounced him I found out I loved him. That's how I cannot forgive myself.'

Maybe it was schadenfreude, although I was moved by the man's honesty, but I couldn't help thinking that my own difficulties were nothing in comparison with Chen's mind games in the Cultural Revolution. When we filmed the Hong Kong director Wayne Wang, who had completed his first US studio film, *The Joy Luck Club*, I had to ask him how he had acquired the name of a Chinatown porn star. He was delighted to answer (I think because the politically correct in the West would not usually ask for fear of discovering that Wayne is a name going back many dynasties). 'My father named me after John Wayne,' he said. I assumed he was joking, but no, he had grown up in Hong Kong named after an American actor who was an unlikely hero there. This followed his role in the 1955 movie, *Blood Alley*, in which he played Captain Tom Wilder, an American who reluctantly ferries a group of Chinese refugees down the Yangtze in a run-down paddle steamer to escape communist China. And now Wayne Wang was directing in America, and he loved it.

The job of television producer does not follow the natural rhythms of life. It can mean long spells as a househusband followed by short spells on what feels like another planet. We edited the London Film Festival programme at a facility in a building called 4 Millbank, which is about a quarter of a mile down the road from the Houses of Parliament and is where all of the major broadcasting organisations have their Westminster studios. Most edit facilities for TV are in Soho, and a large portion of the hourly edit charge is paying their extortionate rent, so 4 Millbank was trying to lure producers of documentaries to its own facilities, which, when there was no big political story, were often idle.

The rates were good and the atmosphere bizarre. If you watch the news on the BBC, ITN, Sky, CNN or just about anywhere, you will see a politician performing an establishing shot walking up some stairs before cutting to a head and shoulders of them being interviewed. This is always 4 Millbank, whose grand building fortuitously looks vaguely parliamentary. Everyone working there came to take it completely for granted that they would follow anyone from Lady Thatcher to Tony Blair up the stairs and end up on the *Nine O'Clock News*. It occurred to me at this time that this could be the perfect moment for me to join the IRA. I wouldn't, of course, even, I believe, if I had been raised in Ireland, but that I could entertain such a thought even in a spirit of levity gave me pause for thought. It was also the first time I wondered if I was eligible for Irish citizenship. (The answer is yes.) There would be two advantages to this: an Irish passport, rendering me the last rather than the first hostage to be shot in a terrorist hijack, and what I had heard were the lavish tax breaks for writers and film people in Ireland.

But 4 Millbank also frustrated me. The deeper I got into the edit the more I wanted to pursue Michael Joseph Brennan and Ann Jones of no known abode. I had nothing to go on but their names, and had no idea whether they married in a hurry and then split up a few years later. Neither did I know whether they were alive or dead, in England or Ireland, America or the Congo. Logically it seemed they might have put down some kind of roots in Blackheath, but unless they had suddenly made an awful lot of money they would not still be there, probably having moved to one of the less expensive areas of London.

My best first reference point was the London phone directory, which listed a number of M.J. Brennans. In a break from the edit late on a Thursday afternoon I phoned four of these numbers with my heart thumping. 'Hello, is Michael there?' was always my opening line. Three of those answering had English accents and no Michaels about the house. The fourth, in the East End of London, had both a Michael and an Irish accent. Unfortunately Michael was still at school playing for the football team. It really was like ringing for John Smith, and I didn't have the hours in the day to engage in any more meaningful research. Once again it felt like an aspect of love, like as a boy meeting at the bus stop an utterly gorgeous girl who, incredibly, seemed to show a flirtatious interest, but then failing to follow her interest up, until the whole thing curdled into lumpen inaction.

When I returned home that evening I discussed my lack of progress with Lydia. She suggested that if we knew Ann was a nurse then surely there was a good chance that she would be registered at the Royal College of Nursing, even if she wasn't still practising. We found a phone number, but then it dawned on me that a deep-voiced man ringing out of the blue hunting a nurse's address would ring alarm bells. Lydia then volunteered to do the job the next day. I felt guilty about this. Involving another person increased my awareness that although some would regard this as innocent and rightful tracing, others would see it as hunting an innocent quarry. I had sympathy with both perspectives. My course of action seemed entirely defensible to me, but I felt less sure about handing it over even partially to someone else.

The next morning we had a huge problem in the edit. When Shashi Kapoor had been interviewed he had arrived wearing a magnificent ivory wrap across his shoulders, the temperature in London being half what it had been for him in India a few days before. Seen through the camera's eye the ivory wrap now looked like a dirty old bedsheet, and my editor suggested that Mr Kapoor had been made to look less like one of the icons of Indian film and more like the subject of a documentary about the down and out.

There are things you can do with video images. I tried to see if we could colourise the wrap to an attractive turquoise and this looked really beautiful, but then we noticed that the whites of Mr Kapoor's famous big brown eyes had also turned turquoise. We tried a distracting tactic by sliding a still from his film into the top right of frame, but since he had been playing an unshaven, destroyed, shadow of former greatness this actually accentuated the homeless image. He looked as if he had arrived at a halfway house.

'Oh what the heck,' I said. 'Leave it as it is.' I went to fetch a couple of cups of tea and phoned Lydia. She had not let the grass grow under her feet, and had made first-rate contact with someone at the Royal College of Nursing. Explaining her errand, she had been careful to say that she wouldn't dream of asking for a contact address, but she was just hoping to find out if there might still be an A.M. Brennan practising as a nurse somewhere in Britain. The lady at the RCN was delighted to confirm that there was indeed an A.M. Brennan practising as a nurse. What was more, there were over forty A.M. Brennans practising as nurses in the United Kingdom. At which point Lydia concluded that it wasn't really worth asking whether, by any chance, there might be an A.M. Jones still nursing.

Lydia had done her bit, I felt, and I tried my one remaining lead myself. I had been told that Ann had been finishing her training at St Giles's Hospital, Camberwell at the time of my birth. During the lunch break that day I decided to phone and see how far I could get. In any organisation there's often an individual who is a sort of living archive. It could be that a nurse who had been a trainee with Ann might now be a senior sister and would remember her from thirty years before. But I hadn't expected that St Giles's had now been integrated into the huge King's Hospital, Dulwich, and no matter how hard I tried there was no way I could make the King's switchboard understand what I wanted. Eventually they put me through to a frosty administrator, and by this time the only card I had left to play was to tell her a précis of the full story and throw myself on her mercy.

She was not impressed. I could tell that her every instinct was to tell me to go away and mind my own business, and I felt that there was some kind of personal agenda for her in this beyond the rightful call of duty. She was as unhelpful as it is possible for one human to be to another. In the end I said, 'Look, please, all I'm asking is that you have a look in your files to see if there was a nurse under either of those two names in 1961, and whether you have any contact for her. All I would want is for someone to forward a letter. Could you just have a look. Please?' The administrator gave a grunt that I took to be a yes. I asked if she would like me to write to her with evidence of my identity to confirm she wasn't dealing with a madman. She said that would not be necessary. I thanked her and gave her three phone numbers for me. She put the phone down. I held out hope for nearly a month but she never phoned back. I realised that I should have left it to Lydia.

The following Monday I was working from home. I reread the notes I had taken in my meeting at the adoption society and realised that I hadn't entirely run out of leads. Certainly I couldn't see what I could do in London, but I had forgotten that at some time between my conception in February 1961 and my birth in November Michael and Ann had married. My rough notes of the meeting even specified that they had been married for about four months before I was born.

The weekend had topped up my batteries. It was not that I had just had a birthday, but that I had scored a goal to equalise for the Cakemaker's Dozen against Sporting London in a match played virtually under water in the mud of Battersea Park. The goal was one that seemed to give my team-mates more pleasure than any I had recently scored. We were one–nil down with two minutes to go and the opposition's left-back muffed a clearance, which I blocked,

took past him and, to everyone's astonishment, walloped
home from an acute angle past a drenched and freezing
goalkeeper. My team-mates loved it not because of any skill
– they have come to regard all my goals as degrees of fluke
– but because it was so bloody English, a goal that arose
from suffering, that snatched honour from the jaws of
defeat. What these Irish people would one day have to come
to terms with is that they had marooned me in a country
who loved nothing better than the spectacle not of a victory
but of a hard-fought draw.

On the Monday, therefore, even sitting down hurt. I
don't understand why the physical effects of a match now
escalate throughout the following week, but I've suffered
enough to know that Monday can be managed with a nap
and a lot of chocolate but it's best not to make any plans
for Wednesday that involve bending, or even walking.
Bolstered by a slab of Cadbury's Dairy Milk and three
mugs of Ceylon tea, I called International Directory
Enquiries to ask if there might be such a thing as a Registry
of Marriages in Ireland. Moments later I was connected to
a place called Joyce House in Dublin. The contrast with
the unhelpful attitude of the administrator at King's was
absolute. It's a terrible cliché, and it can really piss them
off, but it is very hard to avoid the conclusion sometimes
that the Irish are, at first acquaintance, just a friendlier,
more helpful bunch of people. They don't like this assess-
ment if it carries with it a patronising follow-up remark
involving the Blarney Stone or a prolonged anecdote about

being given road directions by an Irishman, but at a moment like this during my first ever telephone call to Ireland on this issue, it could not have made for a happier beginning.

Of course I would not have been the first person to call Joyce House in search of his roots. Apparently they are busy throughout the year dealing with enquiries from thousands of Americans who are not adopted but, knowing that their great-great-grandparents left from Bantry Bay one hundred and fifty years ago, are now seeking to root themselves in the part of Ireland from whence their ancestors originally came, which in many cases they do not know. The man on the phone was very polite about this, but I somehow felt that my enquiry should be nearer the top of his list. I told him precisely what my problem was and followed it up with the following short letter. I had abandoned the non-committal phrasing of the clerk by now and just wanted to put it across without dilution:

I am writing to request a copy of the marriage certificate of my natural parents, and I enclose a sterling cheque for £5.50 to cover your costs. My mother was Ann M. Jones. She would have been born in 1939 (or possibly late 1938). My father was Michael Joseph Brennan. He would have been born in 1931 (or possibly late 1930).

The wedding took place between May and August 1961. It took place in Ireland, but I am afraid I do not know in which county. They left for London soon after the wedding and resided at 48 Lee Terrace, Blackheath, London.

*I do hope you are able to help. If these details are insuf-
ficient, please feel free to telephone me. I should perhaps point
out that I was adopted into a London family soon after I was
born, and my name at birth was Rory Brennan. Many thanks
for your help.*

Yours faithfully

I walked down to the post office with this letter. I wanted
to check that it weighed the right amount for the stamp I
was using, that if ultimately I would hear nothing back it
wouldn't be because the letter had not arrived. Now I had
to wait. I had been told by Joyce House that I should expect
to hear nothing for at least three weeks, and that although
they would do their best it was quite likely that the information I had given them would not be sufficient to lead to
a marriage certificate.

Raised in the Church of England, educated at a C. of E.
school, I had never met an Irish priest. I'd met some
Catholic priests, but only in the precincts of Westminster
Cathedral, London's principal place of Catholic worship.
When I was at school one of our teachers made brilliant
use of a few General Studies classes to stick us in a minibus
and show us some of the architectural contrasts in London,
a city we lived in and yet simply didn't know. On one trip
he took us to Dolphin Square, Pimlico School, Eaton
Square and finally Westminster Cathedral.

There is no building in London that delivers such a shock on the first visit. What from the outside is an unremark-able red-brick cathedral (which looked very like our school) reveals itself when you enter to be only half finished. The lower levels of walls, columns and ceilings are arrayed with marble like melted Neapolitan ice cream, gold leaf and traditional Christian imagery, but looming above is bare brick. Bare black brick. Tons of it, like one of the worst industrial images from *Hard Times*. To the young mind it seemed like a brilliant inversion of the way in which a church is usually trying to direct your imagination. Rather than hell being below and the glories of the heavens twink-ling above, in Westminster Cathedral it looks as if hell has already taken over the heavens, which have slid in defeat towards the ground. Since that first visit I have returned hundreds of times. I wouldn't wish to live without a space in the city in which to go at time of spiritual need. The paradox of Westminster and its vast open space always engage me.

It was at Westminster that I first learned that Catholic priests have all the latest gear. It's well known that their altars, frescoes, stations of the cross and attendance soar above those of the wilting Church of England, but I was still shocked to see that they used microphones. I don't really approve of this, because it seems more than likely that this isn't only to project their voices but allows them to whisper in barely audible tones that, when sent down wires to distant parts of the nave, then slip out of an unseen loudspeaker, like an erotic stranger approaching from behind and breathing rudenesses into one's ear.

Westminster Cathedral also had a constant bustle of activity. It lacked the museum atmosphere of Anglican churches. Maltese ladies with feather dusters were at the crucifixes like fury, flowers were constantly arranged and scrutinised, priests were in and out of confession boxes and giving instructions to men in shiny trousers who didn't seem to have a roof over their heads other than this. I had always read the various Catholic newspapers on my visits, as well as the latest booklets of instruction from the Pope on matters of the soul. Reading that my early use of the British condom was some kind of sin I was content to ignore the religion but enjoy the building. I did not know it, but I was already a lapsed Catholic.

Many thinkers in Ireland passionately believe they do not have the priesthood they want nor deserve. The problem, once again, seems to stem from the Dark Ages. Many believe that with barbarians marauding across Europe at the end of the Roman Empire, Christianity was all but snuffed out and pushed to the westernmost fringes of the north-west European islands. There it was preserved in the enlightened monasteries of Ireland, where, it is said, when the priests weren't illuminating great manuscripts – thereby maintaining the last link between the civilisation of antiquity and the end of the Dark Ages – they were having regular sex with their wives. You will have noticed that this is not an option open to the Irish priest today.

It is argued that with the first glimmering of dawn at the
end of the Dark Age the best of these Irish monks set off
for Europe – a Europe which was entirely unruly and
uncivilised. They soon learned that in order to survive
spiritually and physically while they founded great new
orders, then asceticism must be their ethos. Having reseeded
Christianity in Europe, many of their followers then
returned to Ireland, particularly orders of Augustinians and
Cistercians, *virgo intacta*. They were not keen to let the Irish
monks be otherwise. Taken together with the invasion of
the Anglo-Normans in the twelfth century, what was specifically Irish in Christianity, especially sexual tolerance, was,
it is argued, quashed.

In his excellent account of the Catholic Church in
modern Irish society, Tom Inglis shows how this process
was completed in the last century and how it can be
discerned in the sometimes crude vernacular of the Irish
male, which contrasts starkly with his obeisance in church:

In nineteenth-century Ireland sexual ribaldry was
reduced from the physical to a verbal level. Sex became
a serious subject and the Church developed a monopoly of knowledge about it. Shame and guilt about
sexual practices were instilled in each individual,
privately, in a hushed manner, in the dark isolated
space of the confessional. Sexual morality became a
major issue, but it was wrapped up in a veil of silence.
When it was talked or written about it was in a vague,

abstract, formal language, which prevented the laity from developing any communicative competence about it. The control of sexual knowledge was crucial to maintenance of the Church's power. The humorous references and asides may be understood as unconscious relief mechanisms from a rigid system of sexual supervision and control. Verbal sexual ribaldry, like some of the pagan practices, is a cultural residue of past practices. It appears, like many other aspects of Irish life as ambivalent, and yet relieves tension from rigid norms of social conduct which regulate the relations between men and women.*

Whatever his history, the post-war Irish priest has a status that is beyond comprehension for anyone reared anywhere but the strictest religious households in England. I recently saw a corporate video for an Irish water authority that used some really fascinating archive footage from the time that rural water schemes were first set up in Ireland. I was thrilled to see a 1940s parish hall meeting full of Irish farmers on quite basic but captivating colour film, with the man from the water authority pointing at a blackboard to show them all they'd need to know about sumps and pumps. Next to the blackboard were two important-looking men in dark suits, but sitting in pride

---

* Tom Inglis, *Moral Monopoly – The Catholic Church in Modern Irish Society*. Gill and McMillan, Dublin, 1987.

of place at the centre of the top table was a priest. 'What the hell is the priest doing there?' I asked. 'Jeez, these fellas are everywhere,' was the reply.

The archetypal story of the child given away because of the fear of illegitimacy is a common one, and one known widely throughout my life. I had heard stories dated as recently as the 1970s of women in England and Scotland who were sent to the infamous Magdalene Laundries. There they would give birth to their child, suckle it, have it adopted, and then labour for years under the often punitive supervision of nuns and priests seeing to the dirty laundry of an entire town. Astonishingly, some of these young women would be so institutionalised that, even though they had every legal right so to do, they never got round to leaving until finally the last of these ghastly places was closed. They came to believe that they had indeed sinned against the Lord and that their present condition, up to their elbows in Omo, was no more than they deserved. Perhaps the most heart-rending aspect of these women's stories was that their voluntary incarceration was extended more than anything else because they had been shunned by judgemental relatives in the outside world.

I was aware, therefore, that the population on this side of the Irish Sea had no reason to be proud of the way we had dealt with our own, as they are now called, crisis pregnancies. But still I wanted to do what I could to understand the particular Irish twist on this story. From what I understood, the fact that a bride in England walked down the aisle in the early, indiscernible stage of pregnancy and that a baby was born just six months later was generally excused by the very fact that the sexual partners had got married, even if only at the end of a shotgun. Most English adoptions sprang from the young woman being abandoned by her young man. How could it be that my own Irish natural parents couldn't have held on to their first-born child, even though they were married when I was born?

I found some illumination in a forty-year-old book by an Irish priest, Cecil J. Barrett, CC, *Adoption – The Parent, The Child, The Home*. Father Cecil was directing this book towards Irish Catholic social workers. Like many priests he was not blind to what was happening in the world of the irreligious and he sought to rally the faithful:

The efforts of non-Catholic social workers in other countries on behalf of the unmarried mother are tending more and more to become purely humanitarian. The emphasis is laid on her social and economic difficulties to the disregard of her moral problems. Whilst her fall may be deplored because she has a child to be provided for, only too often it is readily condoned and excused. Her condition is referred to as the unfortunate consequence of a slip or mistake on her part . . . No cognisance is taken of the gravity of sin, or the beauty of the virtue of purity. The very idea of sin would sometimes appear to be outside the ambit of their ministrations. (p.23)

Father Cecil's angle on the unwed mother appears to be paradoxical, for while he urges sympathy he also, almost unconsciously, sanctions betrayal. He reveals himself most fully when he discusses the necessity for secrecy, reminding the Catholic social worker that the revelation of a secret entrusted to them by the young woman is 'a mortal or venial sin according to the gravity of the matter disclosed and the harm thereby resulting to the person whom the secret may concern'.

Reading this one might form the impression that even if the Catholic social worker was going to come down on the woman like a whirlwind at least she would have the consolation of a real confidante. But not exactly, for Father Cecil reasons that there are occasions where this confidence may be broken, for example 'when it is necessary to avert harm from the person confiding the secret, the harm involved may be physical or it may be moral – such as an unmarried mother's fixed resolve to return to live with the father of her baby'.

No guesses here as to who is the best person the social worker should break this confidence to – a priest. The thrust is that it is better that the child be put up for adoption than that the mother returns to the child's father. I have heard many comic tales of priests at dances, monitoring the distance between dancers, especially with the advent of rock n'roll, but oblivious to the couples round the back of the dance hall making love standing up. The kind of manipulative meddling of separating a mother and a child because of the circumstances of the child's conception does not make me laugh at all, however.

Perhaps this is one of the most sinister forms that human behaviour can take – the person, priest or otherwise, who sidles up and makes themselves your friend, your prop in a crisis, and then fells you with a left hook before picking you up again with tender loving care, though exclusively on their own terms and conditions. This repulses me, and yet later in Father Cecil's book I was astonished to find a passage that precisely fitted the circumstances of my own adoption. For with his beady, priestly eye he had noticed that some of his flock conceived illegitimately, married in haste but still gave their child away. His advice to the Irish Catholic social worker is this:

> She [the social worker] will find that the parties are absolutely unwilling to face the shame of a baby being born before its time or even to entertain the idea of keeping it. If they are of the middle-class they will offer the excuse that they are not yet in a financial position to have a normal marriage and to set up home consistent with their class. Their secret must be concealed from parents and friends and they are not prepared to accept any advice contrary to their own plans already made . . .
>
> The worker should point out to them that it is unnatural for parents to get rid of their child. Parents are most strictly bound to provide for the religious,

moral, physical and intellectual education of their
children and to make provision for their temporal
welfare. They are bound to love and maintain them
and they sin grievously if, without real necessity, they
get rid of them . . .

Their future happiness together is intimately linked
up with their first-born and if he has been cast aside
from selfish motives they can have little hope of real
and enduring married bliss. They must not condemn
the innocent victim of their sin to a life amid strangers.
(p.34)

It is not my ambition to pick an argument with a priest
expressing the views of his day. Indeed, I was excited to
find that in this last passage he seemed to have recorded
precisely the dilemma that my own natural parents, from
what I could understand, had faced. To discover this in a
book published just a few years before my birth was reassuring, because it offered an account of how an Irish
Catholic married couple of the period could countenance
giving away their child.

But there is a crucial difference between the order of
priorities Father Cecil gave in raising a child – 'religious,
moral, physical and intellectual' – and the order I knew to
be nearer the mark. By the time I'd read his book two of
our children had been born, and the order of priority for
us was physical, moral, intellectual and, in last place, religious. I want my children to find their own wonder in

Westminster Cathedral, or in Neasden Hindu Temple, but
I will not demand that they fear Westminster Cathedral,
nor that they should kneel or genuflect to any man or
symbol within. Father Cecil was clever enough to have
described my circumstances at birth, but I was the temporal soul who had to live with them. Without his church
those circumstances would not have mattered more than
the name of the month in which I was due. But without
his church I wouldn't have had the filthy black brick arches,
the rippled green and red marble of Westminster. I
regretted no part either of the life I had gone on to lead nor
any quarter of this weird building. But I was beginning to
suspect that if my natural parents were like those legions
of candle-lighters, busy in its many alcoves in mid-
November, regret and guilt would prove to be an inevitable
part of their condition.

Three weeks later to the day, the only item on the doormat
in the second post was a slim white envelope from Ireland.
With its tiny Eire stamp and its wafer-thin proportions, it
made my heart sink even before I had picked it up. I realised
that this single, formal letter from Ireland was going to be
my first major dead end, and I felt a keen sense of disappointment. So different from the philately of England with
its Queen's head – which seemed part of the same deal as
'promising to pay the bearer' on bank notes and her
demand in my passport that in her name I must be allowed
to travel without impediment – that peculiar little stamp

was from a strange land to which I had foolishly allowed myself to imagine I might in some way be connected, a land that was about to reject me without a second thought.

As I do with all special letters, I spent two minutes grazing our mantelpiece to retrieve the silver letter-opener from beneath a pasture of petrol receipts, one-day travel-cards and reminders from Access. Rather than simply jamming my index finger into the top corner and shoving it to the other end I inserted the opener and slid it along with the delicate precision of Mr Darcy opening one of Elizabeth Bennet's scented missives. In my stomach, and I can feel it now, I had stage one symptoms of nausea.

As I had feared, there was just a single sheet of paper within. I unfolded it, my stomach now clenching a little, a bitter taste in my mouth, and saw that Harp symbol that appears on so much Irish paraphernalia. A four-pack of Harp lager used to be the best part of my ritualised, suburban Saturday nights at adolescent parties twenty years before, providing the relaxant to snog someone during the cacoph-onous chorus of 'Nights in White Satin'. (Yes I love you, ahahaagh, Yes I love you, ohhoho, Howwhllayluurrve you, etc., press, snog, fumble.) This is what the Harp logo meant to me, the hopes and fears of teenage years, not a national symbol that was about to deal me a mighty official blow.

Sullenly I allowed my eyes to scan the first line. '*Posadh a Sollunaiodh i i gCeantar Claraitheora i gCeantar Claraitheora Mhaoirseachta i gContae.*' What the bloody hell did this mean? Bastards, they've written to me in Irish. What kind of a useless bunch of historically obsessed, rain-drenched twats begin a word with a small g? Hang on, what's this bit? Oh, sorry Ireland, actually there's a translation in English underneath. Christ, it's the marriage certificate. Isn't it?

I was confused. I rummaged in the empty envelope for a letter or even a compliment slip, but there was nothing. I looked again at the piece of paper that it had contained. It was a marriage certificate. 'Lydia,' I yelled, 'they've found the bloody marriage certificate. Look.' I hope I never live to be too old to bounce up and down on the spot, dancing like a puppet whose strings are being yanked by a class of five-year-olds at moments such as this. This was the breakthrough, this was the detail, this meant, no matter how difficult my quest might be hereon, that I would find them. Alive or dead, I would find them. Before I opened the envelope, I could only say that I came from Ireland, but with the marriage certificate I now knew that the terrified, young Irish couple had faltered their way down the aisle in Rathvilly, County Carlow. Where on earth was that?

The marriage certificate was peppered with new information. Michael Brennan's parents, named on the document, were Patrick Brennan and Mary Broderick. Ann Jones's parents were William Jones and Jenny Finnegan. The witnesses to the wedding were Sean Brennan and Bernadette Jones, who I guessed were probably Michael's brother and Ann's sister. The document also gave Ann and Michael's dates of birth, and I realised that this might eventually be crucial in locating them wherever they might now live, or in the event that they were dead to prove that it was their headstones I had found.

But the one name on the document that I could tell would be crucial was that of Nicholas J. Cullen, PP. To the Anglican mind, PP is the extra charge you pay for postage and packing when you are weak enough to order something from a colour supplement (This lovely garden chair, just £19.99 plus £19.99 P&P). After scratching my head for a while I realised that the signatory on the line beginning 'Married in the Catholic Church of Rathvilly according to the Rites and Ceremonies of the Catholic Church by me Nicholas J. Cullen, PP' must be that of a parish priest.

The search now had a momentum of its own. There may have been one or two doors I could have refused to pass through on the journey thus far, but if I didn't engage with the gift that the arrival of the marriage certificate had given to me I feared that I would end up travelling to the church at Rathvilly and meet not people but ghosts – a vanished man in a futile search for the already departed.

Lydia had one, old and basic Irish guidebook upstairs. Rathvilly didn't make the index, but Carlow did – 'the smallest county in Ireland' and 'the other side of the Wicklow Mountains from Dublin'. Before that second post I had never even heard of Carlow; now I was connected irrevocably with the smallest county in Ireland. It would be quite a boast to have been raised in the smallest house in Ireland, or to have swum the widest lough, or to have baked the fruitiest barmbrack, but I was not sure how the smallness of my county changed my perception of myself. If I was an American roots-searcher, would I not be thrilled by this tiny boast? It didn't seem enough. It was time to call International Directory Enquiries again.

There was no Rathvilly Church listed, but there was a Rathvilly National School. I rang that and asked the lady who answered if she might be kind enough to look up the telephone number for the local church in her phone directory. To my astonishment the number tripped off her tongue with no further reference, which gave me cause to think that this Rathvilly place might not be terribly big.

'Oh, right,' I said. 'You don't happen to know a Father Cullen, I suppose?'

'I do, but I'm sorry to say he has passed away now.'

'Oh, I see.'

The lady evidently caught the disappointment in my voice and went on. 'You could talk to Father Flood though. He took over from Father Cullen.'

'Oh, brilliant, thank you. I'll try him at the church.'

'You won't find him there at the moment. You'd do best to try the parochial house.' Again, Anglican man, what the hell was a parochial house? Was it like a crack house, or a safe house, or a trust house? The concept of a parochial house meant nothing to me.

'Who should I ask for?'

'You'd ask for him but it'll be him that answers the phone in any case.'

'I see. Does he run it then?'

'It's the parochial house. He lives in it.'

'Oh, of course. Do you know the number there?'

Again the number came straight from her memory. I thanked her and rang off. There didn't seem much point in prevaricating further. She was probably already on her way to this parochial house to tell Father Flood that a mysterious Englishman had been asking after Father Cullen. I dialled the number she had given me, which rang in a slightly Agatha Christie way, with a dialling tone of the twentieth-century but only just. Father Flood answered.

'Hello,' I began, 'I wonder if you can help me. I am looking for two people who married in your church in 1961. I don't know where they are now, I don't know whether they've emigrated to America or whether they are alive or dead. I have their marriage certificate and I would be very grateful if you might be able to tell me if they have any relatives living in the Rathvilly area who I might go to to find more information.'

'I'd be glad to help you if I can,' replied Father Flood. 'But, can I ask you, why are you looking for these people?' This was a very difficult question. Uppermost in my mind was what the director of the adoption society had said – that none of my natural parents' relatives knew of my birth or even of my conception. It was critical that I be as discreet as possible. I fudged for a few seconds.

'I'm a relative. Look, actually I'm their son. I'm sorry

about this, I know you're a priest and keeping secrets is part of your job . . . it's just that what I have to tell you is a matter of utter confidence.'

'Yes. Go on.' And so I sang like a canary.

We got along well on the phone, and I followed up with a letter restating my dilemma and assuring him of my need for complete discretion. Christian theology is full of stories of members of flocks being lost and then found, and in being found causing double the rejoicing in heaven. To Father Flood I was about as lost as it was possible for one of his flock to be.

Just before Christmas Father Flood wrote back with this kind and thoughtful letter:

Dear Paul,

I write this short note just to let you know that I have not forgotten you. I have spent quite some time researching and quietly investigating the background to the queries which you have raised. At the moment I am not in a position to give away any details, but I am continuing to pursue the quest and I will be in touch with you again probably sometime after Christmas. Meanwhile I do hope you have a very Happy Christmas and a Wonderful New Year. Trusting that your wife Lydia and Jake and Benjamin are all in good health and keeping you busy caring for them coming up to this Season of Goodwill.

I am yours sincerely,
Edward Flood, PP

Short of sending the letter inside a mince pie, Father Flood could not have written a more seasonal, hopeful letter. Where once I had the symptoms of unrequited love, now I had the constant tingle of expectation of the seeming inevitability of what lay just the other side of Christmas, although winter would turn into spring, and spring into summer before I would hear anything more.

As I write these words at the end of the chapter it is six o'clock in the evening six years to the day since I spoke to Father Flood. The bells at the Catholic church in Lewisham are ringing for a service – dully, repetitively, but as magically to me as the call to prayer from a mosque to a tourist who cannot understand the words but whose heart responds. From the top of my hill I am above the illuminated, blue-dressed statue of Mary that tops the church, and I can look down on her. What a pity she had to be a virgin.

4

A Crystal Palace

JEWISH, or maybe Irish.

In the years before these events, when I was questioned about how it felt to be adopted, I used to say with perfect honesty that I was not aware that being adopted had made or marred my life in any way. This was a boring and disappointing answer, but it wouldn't kill the discussion. Most women at a dinner table would soon laughingly agree that with the surge of hormones of their teenage years they had all fantasised that they might be adopted, had even, at moments of maximum belligerence, yelled at their unfortunate mothers, 'I wish I was adopted,' before storming upstairs into the arms of Leonard Cohen and their dreams of marrying Prince Andrew.

I heard this account as commonly as I heard people laughing about their first spots or kisses. I didn't mind at all, although in some way they seemed to be missing my point, which was so impossible to express that it never once emerged from my mouth. I probably wanted to say, 'No, being adopted hasn't made a difference. But don't you think that is fantastic? That a child can take something so immense in its stride. Can't you see the implication? That we are all indeed born with a clean slate. That we may all become whatever our environment permits us to become if we stick to our guns. That nationality doesn't, mustn't matter. That a bond to one's roots is actually a bondage.'

But I didn't say that. It's a bit pompous for dinner. So I put it another way.

'Well, if I ever did go hunting some roots I would love to be either Jewish or Irish.'

'Why?'

'Because it must be very relaxing to know what you believe in. And because if you want to be a writer you've got a fantastic bedrock to rail against and deny. And because of their observances. That's what I miss by not being Jewish or Irish, their observances.'

By now – and this was the 1980s when confident young men in stripy shirts came straight from their labours in the City of London – a boyfriend of a woman friend, whose choice deeply disappointed me, would focus on me from the end of the table. 'You'd rather be Irish than English [snort]. Don't you like being English?'

This I found hard to answer. The truth was I didn't feel English, because I had never had any contact with what other people felt to be the essence of England. It must have been wonderful to have been raised in the country, to have bellowed 'Jerusalem' at school, to have joined the MCC, to have a string of forebears who'd fought in the Boer, the First and the Second World Wars, to be a remnant of the colonial might that England once exerted across the world.

At my school, however, we were all a bit ashamed of that. There are some easy factors to identify here. Throughout my main school years (1970–1979), England was in accelerated decline, economically, politically, globally, industrially. We failed to qualify for the World Cup even once during that period, and each failure loosened the weave in the national fabric (others have written eloquently and at perhaps unnecessary length about losing to Poland in 1973, but by Christ that hurt the pride of an eleven-year-old).

Across the Channel, we were told, the Germans, to whom we had lost large portions of our cities in two wars, were living off the fat of the land and beginning to tell us how to manage our own economy. In the East, millions of Soviet troops were ready to maraude across Europe, and the map of the city that I called home was daily being scrutinised from a bunker in Latvia for the choicest spot to land one of a thousand nuclear missiles.

The strangulated accents of our ruling class were a world humiliation, nobody believed in God but they still bored for England on the subject, the weather was atrocious, and our underclass was either drunk or smashing each other's heads in at soccer matches. Above all – and this was what really got my goat – we were diabolical at communicating with each other. This England, to me, stank.

I went to school at Dulwich College in south London. It was a huge school, and I enjoyed it. Sending me to it was the best thing my parents could have done for me, because it was a world into which I could daily go, discover, argue, endure, relax and play. The rooted children probably looked forward to going home, as I think my own children do now, but I looked forward to going to school. It sustained me.

Its mix of teachers was bizarre. At one extreme was a regiment of rugger buggers to whom the school was meant to be breeding another generation of insurers and colonial administrators. At the other extreme was a collective of bearded worshippers of D.H. Lawrence, men who would flick their long hair back to reveal a copy of Chairman Mao's *Little Red Book* jutting out of their top pockets. In the middle could be found science teachers who were half man, half test tube, men doing their Ph.D.s by correspondence, others undergoing full nervous breakdowns, an assortment of rather poorly concealed homosexuals, about fifteen professed and practising Christians, an art teacher who looked like Jason King and another who was the world's most fastidious man. Most of them were superb teachers. A Dulwich headmaster had to be called the Master, a nomenclature whose credibility was lost when Jon Pertwee's Dr Who sent Roger Delgado's forkbearded, galactic rotter spinning into outer space every Saturday night.

At the time I was there Dulwich College was nearing the end of a post-war educational project known as the Dulwich Experiment. At its peak more than 80 per cent of the boys had been given free places by their local authorities. The Master would parade at the Headmaster's Conference as the head of a great, certainly huge, public school, most of whose pupils would certainly not have cut the mustard at the Henley Regatta. For he drew his ranks of 1,400 boys not from the Home Counties, but from Orpington, Bromley and Beckenham.

Each day a sea of these children would travel up the railway line to West Dulwich station and migrate back to the suburbs every night. And, unlike most public schoolboys, these children would go to Saturday night parties where deeds were done that, now I have my own children, make the hair on the back of my neck stand up. A small minority of the boys would take the opportunity of their daily train journey to slash luggage racks and seats with knives, remove lightbulbs that were then smashed against the live rail, and urinate out of the window into the face of unfortunate passengers leaving the office early two compartments downwind. The Flower of England.

When I arrived at university, one of my earliest acquaintances was a young man called Rupert, the first real Rupert in green wellington boots I had ever met. I described to him the lie of the land at Dulwich, and went on to tell him that during my final year, when I had assumed the unpopular mantle of Captain of School (I know, you don't have to hiss), I had initiated a move to have prefects elected rather than appointed behind closed doors. Rupert, nineteen going on ninety, from Winchester, spluttered on his pipe. 'Good Lord, d'you mean a meritocracy? How corrupt.' It took me ten years to understand his point and ten more to have formulated an argument against it. By now Rupert was probably a monumentally wealthy merchant banker and I doubt he would care.

The kind of equivocal Englishman I was back then had a direct bearing on the way in which I would later receive the news that I was Irish. The Irish, who feel they have reason to believe that the English have not always dealt them from the top of the deck, have been delighted to delegate political power to the European Community in return for its protection and a strong voice in the Council of Ministers. In England, to hold a similar view that to subsume national sovereignty into a greater European state is in the greater interest of general equality is regarded by most of the press as the talk of quislings and self-aggrandising bureaucrats.

Recently I discovered one of those photographs from the past that delivers such a potent shock that it expresses more than a thousand words. It was a turn of the century black and white photograph taken due south from the main rugby pitch at Dulwich, with the cricket pavilion in the middle foreground. A photograph taken today would show that beyond the pavilion in foreshortened perspective are more playing fields, rising in the lower background to the ancient

Dulwich Woods, to be topped in mid-frame by the BBC transmitter aerial for most of London, which looks like a cut-price Eiffel Tower; it's ugly and dominant and ceaselessly transmits the message of the day to the populus below. A message that is unsure of itself, programmes that can be both very good and very bad, a transmission smitten with doubt, perhaps even of paralysis, while the best of us slump below, absorbing the cathode rays.

The old photograph taken from the identical point showed the pavilion, the foreshortened playing fields, the ancient Dulwich Wood and no transmitter mast. In the modern photograph the girders of the transmitter would fill about ten per cent of the top half of the frame, but in this old photograph ninety per cent of the top half of the frame was filled with the immense glass structure of the Crystal Palace. I had had no idea of what a mammoth presence that building would have been before it burned down in 1936. In the photograph it looked as if someone had put the *Titanic* in dry dock on top of the hill. I was so struck by it that I found more photographs taken from Sydenham and Penge, on the other side of the hill, and there it loomed over the terraced houses like a glass cathedral from another planet.

For ten formative years I had gazed at the functional transmitter tower out of classroom windows in a school where doubt was part of the curriculum. But what if I had gazed out at the Crystal Palace, probably moss-covered by then, but perhaps still filled with some of the artefacts of

the Great Exhibition of 1856? A place we would undoubtedly have been taken to on school trips, a place where we
could have seen our past, in its shame and glory. It would
have been a place to go, filled with a tangible bedrock of
conviction. How wonderful to rebel against that, rather
than against the straw dolls of the images of our ruling class
that we would see on taped transmissions fired over our
heads from the Crystal Palace mast.

Five months had gone by since Father Flood's Christmas
letter, but all had been silence.

Dear Father Flood,

*I am writing following our correspondence towards the end
of last year, and wondering if you have been able to discover
any news of the whereabouts of my natural parents. As the
World Cup draws nearer and with the English lion vanquished
yet again I, like millions of others, (and most of the players)
am striving ever harder to find a genetic excuse to support
Big Jack's team.*

*More seriously, I am likely to be visiting Ireland in a month
or so to visit a friend's cottage, and I am trying to establish
whether it might be worth passing through Rathvilly (under
heavy disguise) or pursuing a few separate enquiries in Dublin.
I really would be very grateful to hear if you have heard of
any news of people still in your area who might be related to
me, and most particularly if there is any news of the ultimate destination of Ann Jones and/or Michael Brennan. If*

*you have met only with dead ends I quite understand, but
would appreciate it if you could find time to let me know.*

Yours sincerely.

Father Flood replied swiftly:

Dear Paul,

*I received your letter recently and am glad to see you are
well and trying to hitch on to Jack's army for the summer. I
hope we are not totally disappointed!*

*Since my last correspondence with you I have been very
busy, culminating with Confirmations last Thursday which
required much preparation. However, I do expect to be able
to pursue my investigations for you now, and I'll be in touch
with you again before mid-June.*

*With apologies for my lack of communication in recent
months, I am yours sincerely.*

These two letters were matching pairs, and not just
because of their feeble jokes about the Irish soccer team
about to depart for the World Cup in the United States,
leaving England behind yet again. They were matching
because both of us were not being entirely frank. Lydia and
I do have friends with a house on the Dingle peninsula, but
we had no plans to go there. I didn't even know what or
where the Dingle peninsula was. I'd felt justified though
in turning up the heat by a couple of gas marks, hinting at
the prospect of this blast from the past roaming through

County Carlow, beating his chest with anguish and betrayal.

Father Flood, too, was taking a line rather than being completely frank. At this time he knew rather more than he was letting on, but he had good reason for playing a waiting game.

I treasure my letters from Father Flood. My phone call to Joyce House, my phone call to the Rathvilly National School and my contact with Father Flood had all been warm and amusing encounters. They seemed to bode well, as my first communications with a homeland I did not know. During this time I was used to telling people that I knew nothing about Ireland whatsoever, but on thinking deeper about that statement it began to strike me that this was actually a false premise. On reflection, I had had many interactions with the Irish before I knew I was Irish myself.

A few weeks ago I had the fourteenth and final filling in the surgery of my new, pain-free, female dentist. As I lay back with her assistant doing something I still don't understand with a mini-Hoover, Angela excavating huge chunks from underneath my teeth, I relaxed to the music they were playing by The Corrs. The reason I had to have fourteen fillings in five appointments over many weeks was that I hadn't been to the dentist since 1979, the year I left school. It seems unkind to blame Mr O'Brian for this – I've scored a lot of Mr Kipling's cakes in the intervening twenty years – but he cannot be entirely without guilt.

Mr O'Brian was the first Irishman of my childhood. His reception room in Bromley, a hall of terrors for me, proudly displayed the many trophies he had won as an Irish middleweight boxing champion. He was a very solicitous man and gave many reassurances: 'This won't hurt now, Paul,' or 'Spit that blood out now, Paul, and we'll be away again in a minute.' If I have to do an Irish accent today, it is always Mr O'Brian's that comes up my throat, and the words, 'Open wide now, Paul' inevitably follow. The many Irish people I have come to know in recent years often have a fear of a particular priest. So what, I say – imagine a priest with a drill and no anaesthetic. I can still see the hairy hands and smell the carbolic coming towards my tender young gums.

The very moment I left home I dropped from Mr O'Brian's list, refusing to acknowledge the sinister appointment cards that followed me around the country. I vowed never to sit in a dentist's chair again. With fourteen holes I realised this year that I might soon have more hole than tooth, and I couldn't believe it when the blessed Angela proved, to my stupefication, that it is possible to do a filling without it being a near-death experience. For, although I may not have suffered a pandybatting by a Jesuit priest, my enamel has been mercilessly drilled by his hairy, boxing champion cousin, a man whose fists had formerly smashed the jaws of Irishman from the north and the south into shattered submission.

Mr O'Brian was the only Irishman in my early years of

childhood with whom I came into regular contact. Our black and white television set, though, was bursting with them. Val Doonican, The Bachelors and Dana never did it for me, though Phil Lynott of Thin Lizzy was one of the great talents of the music business – Irish and black.

Oddly, I went on to meet by chance a trio of renowned Irishmen. The first of these I met, but did not know. At Exeter University I did the job of Arts Chairman, importing all sorts of theatre, dance, mime and poetry on to campus. I loved that job, although it was a nightmare to manage while also studying, and it had the huge advantage of giving me an office and secretarial support from a fine Exonian called Betty. I shared the office with King Campus himself, Hugh the Social Secretary, the sabbatical man whose job it was to book and arrange the visiting rock bands.

My job was highly arty-farty, but Hugh was surrounded by a moody tribe of men wearing long black coats, known as the men in black, and was forever working an angle. One week, while I was promoting the mime artist David Glass, Hugh was promoting a rock band apparently so huge that he could run a beneath-the-counter 'guest list', the takings from which I understood assisted Hugh and his girlfriend to further their French studies on a trip to Paris. I liked Hugh and we appreciated each other's work, the difference between us being that I was getting paid not a bean and he was doing just fine.

So it was that on the day of this mega-concert, about which the whole campus was abuzz, I walked into my cherished office to see a greasy-haired man with a big hooter and shades sitting at my desk, using my phone. 'What the—?' I began.

'I'll be done in a moment,' said the greaser, in a thick Irish accent. 'I'm just phoning home.'

It was apparent to me that home meant an overseas call to Dublin, the cost of which would come from my parsimoniously preserved Arts Committee budget. I was not a happy arts tsar, and became actually livid to see that there was another oily, bejeaned, earring-wearing geezer stretched out in his leather boots on Hugh and my sofa, which was usually reserved for his girlfriend and my Arts Treasurer, with whom I shared a close working relationship.

'Come on,' I said, like Parky the Park-keeper, 'off that phone now.'

The Irishman wound up his call and stood slowly. 'I'm sorry, is this your phone? They told us it would be all right.'

By now I knew who this two were – a pair of sponging roadies for this rock band, chancing it in my office. The one on the sofa raised himself, 'Do you know where we can get a drink?' he asked.

Puffing my chest out I said, 'Yes, in the Ram Bar like everyone else. Excuse me.' Making sure that they had gone from the exclusive heights of Top Corridor, the seat of power, I sat down at my desk, wiped the phone with my sweatshirt, and began to prepare the ticket stubs for David Glass. A moment or two later Hugh breezed in.

'Were they up here?'

'Who? What, the roadies? Look, Hugh, if you're going to let them use our office can you tell them to use *your* phone.'

'Sure, all right. Sorry.' He looked thoughtful. 'What happened?'

'I told them to piss off.'

'Paul, what? Bloody hell, mate, they weren't roadies, they were the band. Didn't you know who they were?'

'No,' I replied, beginning to doubt the rectitude of my actions.

'Don't you know who Bono is? Did he have someone with him?'

'Yes.'

'He's The Edge. For Christ's sake, Paul, he's the best guitarist in the world.'

Bonio was a biscuit we fed our dog at home, the edge was the line that defined the extremities of an object, and U2, which I thought to be a pretty silly name, was a famous American spy plane. Later that night, as I walked with the Arts Treasurer up one of the campus's many steep hills, we could hear this U2 playing something called 'The Joshua Tree', which soared through the cold, misty night air. Pah, I thought. That night I didn't even know that I still hadn't found what I'm looking for.

A few months later I was delighted to light the cigarette of another Irish icon. 1983 was not the best of times for The Boomtown Rats. It had been a long time since 'I Don't

Like Mondays', and Bob Geldof's mouth, which had once so appealed to the *NME*, was earning him a full-scale backlash. For the Rats, Exeter was another campus gig, following a trail well-beaten by other bands from whom the heat had departed but who were still well liked – Elvis Costello, Ian Dury, Squeeze and, of course, Gary Glitter.

The band had been doing a sound check, and it was still mid-afternoon. Bob was sitting on the ground at the back of the Great Hall, his long back leaning against a loading bay door. I happened to be walking past on the way to the Northcott Theatre, where I had naive-impresario business to do and he and I were alone.

'Have you got a light?' he said.

I offered him my Swan Vestas, and then realised that he was probably marooned on the campus until the gig.

'Keep them,' I said.

He thanked me.

'Hope it goes well,' I said.

'Yeah,' he replied, with the exhausted manner of one who didn't much like Mondays to Sundays inclusive if it involved retreading old hits for a bunch of student wankers. Eighteen months later he was setting up Band Aid.

The final member of my Irish Trinity was a man who had scared me as a child much more than Mr O'Brian. I've spoken about this man to lots of friends and they have all confirmed that his appearances on English television from the 1960s onwards would actually give them nightmares. I've also spoken to many Irish people about the events with which he was concerned. I am convinced that they have no concept of how shit-scared a lot of young Londoners were by the violence of the IRA, to which this man was passionately opposed but whose embers he seemed ever determined to stoke with his considerable fury. Living in Belfast can have been no cakewalk, but for many of my generation the ease with which Irish terrorists took life in the capital (and other English cities) was as much a factor as the three-day week and the nuclear threat in making us seriously doubt the worth of the country in which we lived.

The IRA were faceless, as were the Unionist terrorists, but while the nationalist cause was represented on our screens by moderately demeanoured men such as John Hume, the Unionists were represented by the Reverend Dr Ian Paisley. His projection of the words 'Utterly', 'Categorically', 'Sin', and 'Antichrist' into my sitting room on a Sunday evening, as I sat watching telly with my parents before *The Onedin Line*, seemed to come from a hellish world of intolerance where denunciation was a field sport. It was like a throwback to my lessons about Guy Fawkes, riddled with wild paranoia about the 'Papistry'.

So I adored the moment twenty years later when I was on my way back from doing some filming at the Royal Shakespeare Company in Stratford and pulled in for a leak at a service station on the M40. I washed my hands and emerged into an open area with a little café called something like Pam's Pantry, and there, sitting at a table

like a bloated vulture come to earth, was the Reverend
Ian Paisley. Set before him on the Formica table was a
mound of cream cakes, which he was devouring at speed
with a well-wielded fork. A photograph then, or better
still an etching by Hogarth, would have been captioned
with one word – 'Gluttony'.

Seated either side of Paisley, their hands not far from the
sinister bulges beneath their jackets, were two Special
Branch officers. I had stopped in my tracks at the sight of
this cholesterol-fest, and one of the officers took note. Now
that I know I look Irish, I don't blame him. I caught his
eye – clearly I wasn't carrying any Semtex – and while
holding his gaze I flicked my eyes quickly across to the
rapidly diminishing pile of sponge and then back to the
officer, before looking heavenwards with an emphasis that
I hoped said, 'What a pig.'

The officer also looked at the cakes, at Paisley, who had
eyes only for his plate, and then back at me, shooting me
a brief but broad grin of complicity. 'Isn't he just?' he
seemed to say. 'And I've got to give my life for this.' Never
mind succumbing to the Papistry, Ian, I wanted to cry,
someone should have warned you about the pastries.

Because of work in television I have come across quite a
few of the famous in the flesh, from Pavarotti to Sharon
Stone, but Ian Paisley is the one emblazoned at the front of
my mental scrapbook. I never saw Pavarotti eat, although
it's not difficult to guess he gets through a few bowls of
pasta, but this would not have affected my judgement of his

wonderful voice. But seeing Paisley, whose utterances had so scared me as a child, cramming that same mouth with empty calories was my number one celebrity catharsis. Ian Pastry.

At about 8 p.m. on the evening of Saturday 4 June, Lydia and I were in the sitting room downstairs about to enter that period of the parental day known as non-persistent vegetative state. Ten years before, on a summer Saturday we would both have been painting some town red, but now, having performed the nightly bath–story–bed ritual for our boys, we were, like them, losing the battle with our tired eyelids.

And then the phone rang. We were a couple of years ahead of most of our friends in having children, and it was always comforting to know that somebody else was also doing nothing on a Saturday night and resorting to the easy stimulation of a phone call. I picked up.

'Is that Paul?'

'It is. Is that Father Flood?' This wasn't a difficult guess. There was no reason for any other Irish voice to be coming down my telephone.

'Were you after getting my letter?'

'Yes, I did. Thank you very much.'

'Well, look, I'm just really sorry that I wasn't in touch for such a long time.'

At that moment I was completely composed. Father Flood, however, seemed to have a heavy cold, have had a couple of drinks, or be holding back some sobs. 'Anyway, I have some news for you.'

The atmosphere in our sitting room suddenly seemed to become more dense, to emit a discernible, low-level, electric hum. My mouth went dry, my heart raced, just as it had when I was under starter's orders for the hundred metres at school. In that briefest of moments I prepared myself for a couple who'd divorced after my birth, headed for different countries, considered their life and their love ruined by my arrival and my disposal, and who had told this poor priest that he must deal with me because they had no intention of acknowledging that I had ever drawn breath.

He continued. 'I'd better not say anything more now.' Jesus, I can't take much more of this, I thought. Not more waiting, please. 'Because I've spoken to the man in question.'

'Who do you mean?'

'I've spoken to the man who is your natural father.'

The starter's gun fired and I was off. The blood to my brain surged and pounded. 'You've spoken to him. When?'

'I'm just off the phone from him now. Have I done the right thing?'

I was very surprised to be asked this by a priest, but he was obviously very shaken by what he had found himself involved in. I felt more like the priest and he seemed more like the man in my confessional box. 'Of course you have. Are you all right, Father?'

'I am, yes. Well, the man in question has said he's prepared to speak with you on the phone. Will I give him your telephone number?'

'Yes. Please do.'

'All right, I'll ring him back now. He's said he'll proba-bly call you tonight.'

'Tell him I'll be here. Thank you, Father. This is very kind of you.'

'No, it's nothing. Well, God bless you, my son.'

'Yes. And you too.'

'Goodbye then.'

That night, however, no phone call came. At about midnight Lydia and I gave up and went to bed, plugging a phone into the socket by our bed in case this man in ques-tion decided to call me after pub closing time from a phone box in . . . in where? I didn't know who he was, where he was, what he would say, what he would want, where this might lead.

At about two in the morning I fell asleep and dreamed about this man, vividly. He was a feckless, unshaven, alcoholic wreck, who barely remembered that he had got married at all. He was somewhere near Birmingham in my dream, and he was going to use my surname and phone number to find my address. He was then going to come round and demand money, threatening our children if I did not yield to him. The dream was so vivid that when I woke up in the morning I felt it with the force of a real experi-ence. And although it had been the first nightmare I'd had

in years it somehow armed me for this call from this man
if and when he ever made it.

At about 10.30 a.m. on Sunday 5 June the phone rang.
I heard the voice of a second Irishman. 'Is that Paul
Arnott?'

'Yes.'

'My name is Michael Brennan. I understand you've been
trying to contact me.'

At which point Jake and Benjamin, by my feet, cracked
heads and jointly began a banshee wail.

'You've got kids?'

'Yes, two boys.' (Stereo screaming.) 'Look, can I give
you another number for my office upstairs. I can't really
hear you.'

'Sure, go ahead.'

We rang off. I gave the boys fifteen seconds' emergency
solace, which worked because they knew I meant it and
meant it very fast indeed. I headed for the stairs, yelling at
Lydia to get out of the bath and get downstairs with the
boys, and soared in my boxer shorts up three flights in one
breath. I crash-landed in my swivel chair and waited for
the phone to ring. Which is when it occured to me that the
man in question might have just used his last ten pence in
the call box, or might have regarded the intervention of two
bawling kids as divine and might now be finding many
sound reasons not to bother phoning back at all. But the
man I had already spoken to had not sounded like the man
in the dream. Neither had he sounded like my second

conscious expectation, a languorous Irishman – the stereo-
typical charmer with the voice of a radio actor. He had
sounded direct, straight. And Irish.

But this time I didn't have to wait thirty-three years, six
months, one night or even one minute for the call. I had
just begun to wring a trickle of ink from a half-spent biro
when the office phone rang.

'Are the kids all right?'

'They are.'

'I knew you had them two boys. The priest told me a
little of your story.'

'He did? Good.'

'I have a lot to tell you. But there's one thing I have to
tell you first. We'd never forgotten you.'

'Right.' The line went a little quiet and I was worried
that I was about to have another grown Irishman going soft
on me on the phone. 'Er . . . where are you?'

'I'm in work at the moment. You can imagine this has
come as a big thing for us, so I'm making this call away
from home.'

Us?

'You're at work, on a Sunday? What do you do?' So
English, so change-the-subject.

'Ah well, I don't know how you stand on this type of
thing. I'm a trade union leader.'

An instant and unexpected fissure of pride shot through
me. That faded shadow of my own radicalism became
momentarily more inky black. 'You're a union leader.

Bloody hell. I was a Marxist myself for a whole year. Although that was 1976.'

'Well and much maligned Marx is and the terrible things that were done in his name. But look, I just wanted to tell you, from my heart, that I'd always sworn that when I retired I would come back to England and find you. No matter what the cost or how long it took. I hope you can forgive us for what we did to you.'

(That 'us' again.)

'What I'm about to say to you is from *my* heart,' I said. 'I have had a wonderful life. I have two parents who've done all they could to take care of me. I have a wonderful wife, who I fell in love with like the whole thing was a miracle, and we have two lovely boys. I'm really glad to hear from you, and I want to hear a lot more, but you have to remember this. Don't blame yourself for anything, because from where I'm standing you have nothing to blame yourself for. If I were to blame you for anything it would be like me saying that my whole life had been a mistake, some kind of terrible disappointment, and believe me, from the bottom of my heart, I believe my life to have been the precise opposite.'

'That's very good to hear. You see . . . we didn't know what you wanted. We've had a fair bit of trouble of late . . . This will sound stupid to you, we didn't know if it was all a punishment for what we did to you.'

Who is we? I thought.

'God, no. The opposite. Someone said one of our kids

looked like me and that made me think about who I looked like. I said this to Father Flood – it just seemed wrong that whoever gave birth to me wasn't allowed to know what had happened to me.'

'The priest said that. He said that you sounded like a very good fellow altogether and we had nothing to fear.'

'Can I just ask you something? Who is we?'

'She's a very good woman, your mother. She's a very kind person, one of the best. I have to be really careful in all this because of her. That's why I'm in work, like I said. I'm in Dublin, did the priest tell you that?'

'No, he told me nothing. I didn't even know whether you were calling from Ireland or America. You've got a blank sheet at this end. Are you telling me you're still married?'

'I thought you knew that.'

'To Ann?'

'Yes. And now here's the good bit. I think you might like this from the sound of you and you being a family man yourself. There are four more of you.'

'You've got more children?'

'Sure, mind they know nothing about you at all, no one does, but let's hope that can all change. Well, there's Liam, and he has two lads himself, Finian and Donnacha, well he'd be not even two years younger than you. He did his apprenticeship like me and he's an electrician now.'

'I'm going to write this down. Is that okay with you? If I've gone silent it's not because I've stopped listening.'

'You do that, that's why I'm on the phone to you. Then there's Maeve, who's your only sister. She's a marvellous girl, but she's had this terrible illness. She's lost a third of her stomach to the cancer. But it's looking good now for her, sure enough. We heard something of you a while back and it was when she was still dreadful ill with the chemo and that. But anyway, she's on her way back up now. She lost all her hair, which was wonderful and dark like your mother's, but it's growing back. She'll be fine. She's in marketing and speaks a lot of languages.'

The impact of this was immense. Having a brother was an extraordinary enough development – one that I had completely overlooked as a possibility on this journey – but having a sister . . . A female, made from the same stuff as me. And a sister I had quite evidently very nearly lost without ever knowing. Even so early on, the thought of having never known about her chilled me to the marrow.

'Then there's Barry, who's a very bright lad. He's just graduated from Trinity. Have you heard of that?'

'Sure, Dublin. What did he read?'

'Law and he's done very well. I'm going to see if there's anything I can do for him through the union. And there's Shane. Now there's an incredible thing because isn't Shane six foot four at the last measurement and I swear he's still growing. Mind, if you saw what he eats you'd see why. He's into the corporate videos and he does the weddings as well. Just starting out, but he's the businessman of us.'

'So, can I just check this? You and Ann are still married

and you have four children? And all of them are directly related to me by blood?'

'They're the same as you, all right. Mind, they haven't got that voice of yours. You sound very English. I don't know – was it Surrey where you were raised?'

'No, not Surrey, no. Sort of Kent, well, south London really. But I went to school in a place called Dulwich.'

'That's an amazing thing, because isn't that where Ann did her training as a nurse.'

'Well, if you think that's amazing, do you remember a place called Blackheath?'

'I remember that all right. That's where Ann had a flat when you were born.'

'If I go to my front window I can see the church spire you and Ann could have seen from Lee Terrace.'

'Is that the case? Isn't it incredible how this whole thing is coming together? Maybe there's somebody looking over us after all.'

For another hour we talked on, with two subjects animating Michael more than any others – children and politics. I think he believed out of instinct that I was fascinated by all shades of the latter, and loved the former. And I think he sensed that because I had children of my own the wheel had turned enough for him to allow himself and his wife to rejoin this circle of life at a point where they would do themselves, their family and me no harm.

That afternoon, Ann phoned. Cautious, shy, sad, seeking meaning, wondering why now. I find it impossible to recall with accuracy what she said, because she worked at a completely different level to Michael. He had been interrogative, positive, clear-cut. She was more like a mother deer who was smelling the damp fur of a newborn for the first time. It was all about sensing, not saying. In moments she was funny, but at others she was pained. For decades she had suffered the loss of the baby who became me in deep silence. Mere words on a phone call from Dublin to London would never suffice to lift it.

Lydia had walked around me with great delicacy that Sunday, but she was bursting to know what they were like. I told her the truth, that I didn't know. I asked, hypothetically, if she would mind if I went to Dublin one weekend to meet them. She smiled, and said of course not. But deep down I was concerned that she would worry that the husband who would return from Dublin could be a changed man from the one she had agreed to marry.

5

Most Obscenely and Courageously

THERE'S an unwritten century stretching ahead of us, and we already know from the ending of the last one that there are dozens of civil wars between ethnic groups still to be fought by men not yet born. I have a fond fantasy, about a new United Nations special peacekeeping unit to be deployed alongside conventional peacekeeping forces everywhere from the Balkans to the Punjab. The sole qualification for membership of this special force, the People's Illegitimates, is that you should have been adopted. At moments of the highest tension in a negotiation between feuding parties, a few members of the P.I. would enter the command tent in a remote forest and reveal their special skills.

'We have two messages for the people of both sides in this conflict,' we would begin. 'First, we were born to one family, even one nation, but raised by another family, and even another nation. We know deep within ourselves this means, beyond refutation, that there are human qualities that supersede bonds of race, nation and even family. Highest of these qualities is the vision to work daily to ensure the peace and welfare of all under law, their origins regardless.'

The unshaven men of violence in the forest would become confused as we walked towards them without fear. (I think our uniform would be diaphanous, like the peacenik creatures from some utopian planet in *Star Trek*.) We would click our fingers and human holograms would appear on either side of each of us. 'And here is the second thing,' we would say. 'Look, to my right. Here is the mother who loved and raised me. She is English. And look to my left, the mother who bore me. She is Irish. What am I? Which one of these mothers is not mine? Under law there is no need for me to choose.'

The unshaven ones, mostly raised in matriarchal societies themselves, would find their eyes filling with sentimental tears. 'Then why must you Serbians/Albanians [delete as applicable] force your people to fight, and teach your children to hate the Serbians/Albanians [delete as applicable]?'

One of the militants would probably then step forward, utter a prayer, and shoot us, saying we were Nowhere People, an offence to God/Allah. This seems to be the standard response from zealots to those whose belief is the belief in no belief. But, luckily, the UN would have given us bulletproof vests and we would continue. 'Look at our lives, look how we compromised. And see how far it has taken us in the understanding of the plights of others cursed to be bound by the delusions of race, ethnicity, nationality or by the blind loyalties of some families.'

What do you think? Not a bad way to die. Unshaven Slobodan would be determined to find a way through our vests in the end, even if it cost him his own life; he'd have too much to lose. Next time Jesus comes back, the twist should be not that his mother was a virgin, but that he was adopted. Then, Temple-goers, see what a really difficult little bastard that would be.

Haven't we put up with enough, though, those of us who've been adopted at birth and lived on thirty, forty, fifty years? Haven't we reached an age where the open window of self-determination should be ours if we wish to look through it, a sort of loyalty bonus? We've all been carrying this hidden burden, which some have borne lightly and some have made our excuse. Is it not we, then, who should decide how we go about unslinging that burden from off our backs, we who should unpack it and see without fear or judgement what lies within?

The tragedy is that not everyone shares this view. I was far enough into the unravelling of this tale now to realise that this was the second checkpoint at which I must consider whether now to tell my (adoptive) parents what was happening. But what was I to do about these proud people, who had adopted me and raised me and loved me? Was I to pop round the next day, tell them the story so far in a breezy fashion and promise to keep them appraised? What if it had not worked out with these new Irish strangers, if it went, as I still expected, no further than my original intention – to give a mother (and now a father) the news that I was alive and well and not planning to haunt their afterlives? This cliché had never applied to me so well before, but I was damned if I did and damned if I didn't.

I admit now that I have developed a fear that has become an aversion and then a total resistance to the censorious who suck their teeth and insist that any adopted child was lucky not to have been brought up in an orphanage, that it had incurred dues that were to be paid in the form of doors being kept locked, bonds remaining eternally dissolved. Until everyone was dead.

The sensibility of being adopted means that you resist thinking like this, resist paralysis of the mind, the deliberate choice to deny, because you know – and you do know it more profoundly than the non-adopted – that these repressions, this unending ledger of duty, is not what our maker would ever have wished. It's a ghastly mental kink, like masochism. As Blake, the son of a Rathmines' boy himself, wrote, be very wary of those mind-forged manacles. It's obvious, isn't it? If you love someone, set them free (Sting, I know, but that doesn't mean it isn't true).

In the last few years I have met other adopted people who have traced their natural parents, and they have come from a great variety of backgrounds, from those adopted into aristocracy to those adopted into working-class foster families. None of them had involved their adoptive parents in their search until they had the full picture, often not until there had been a meeting with the natural parent. The adoptive parents' reactions had ranged from the delighted let's-extend-the-family, ideal response, to never-darken-my-door-again fury. Meanwhile, friends and observers may have sat on the touchline making judgements on how the adoptee had conducted their relationship with their adoptive parents during this time. In my own experience, living in England where the kind of enlightened contact practices introduced in Australia (of which more later) just don't exist, it was an impossible call. I decided not to involve my adoptive parents at this point, and I believe that this was my right.

One of the joys of writing this book was the hundreds of hours spent in the British Library attempting to read every book or paper ever written about adoption. The building of the new British Library has been a well-recorded debacle in the United Kingdom, but the resultant place is a wonder. I am not proud to be British (neither am I unproud), but I am proud to be a citizen of a country that can provide free access to such a living brain, a repository of all that has been written and all that one day will be written. And I was lucky that on the first of many days spent in that hive of industry I found in one book an expression of all the views about adoption that I knew to be wrong.

Here are the notes I fired into the innocent keyboard of my laptop once I had put that book down:

First book opened at the British Library and I already find myself sorely provoked. Alice Heim is/was a Hampstead/ Newnham psychologist and mother of two grown-up adopted children. In her 1983 account Thicker than Water? – Adoption, Its Loyalties, Pitfalls and Joys *she has sent out letters to a small number of adoptees and adopters, who have replied as best they can, only to endure her self-satisfied footnotes and back references. Finally my patience snapped when she gave space to the idea that children not matched to parents from the same social class might cause extra trouble, as if class is some fleshy, all pervading psychic trait handed down through the genes. Her stupidity on this made me wonder what other views she was hiding.*

In general adoptees unthinkingly accept their parents' habits and manners in childhood but, in adolescence or adulthood may come to reject them, especially if their biological parents come from a very different background. In particular their choice of companions and of idioms may become more and more divergent from those of their parents (as seen in Mrs Cypress's account). When this phenomenon occurs in biological families the change in behaviour is often temporary; it is liable to occur as part of the normal teenagers' expression of independence; and when they reach adulthood these young people will often

*embrace once again the values of their biological parents
. . . This reversion to type – if it can be so designated
– works in both directions. Phyllis Crabtree's account
of her experiences of being adopted by someone less
middle class than her biological parents suggests that the
malaise resulting from such disparity may well work both
ways.*

If I juxtapose this idiocy, from a psychologist of all people,
with the barbarism of The Jerry Springer Show I have the
raw material to show, to begin to show, that my deeply held
belief in the absolute essentiality of treating all persons every
day with complete openness and generosity becomes validated.
In other words, it is not the vaguely benevolent waffle of a
confused English Irishman, it is the seedling ground of an
ethos, which as its first premise says death to snobs and cynics!
There, I feel better now. Did I forget to mention that she
allows the idea that 'bad stock will out' to come from the
mouths of others even more entrenched than herself? It came
as little surprise therefore to read on page 102:

*A further point on which I differ from officialdom
concerns the law making it mandatory to allow adopted
offspring to trace their natural parents . . . I believe
after having devoted much time and thought to the
question that this law was ill-conceived. I did not at first
hold this view, realising that it was drafted by well-
meaning people with the interests of the adoptee in mind,*

but I now believe them to have been mistaken. (I am not personally involved in this issue, as neither my son nor my daughters have ever evinced the slightest desire to contact their biological parents.) On exploring the matter I gain the impression that seeking out the biological mother may prove disruptive both to her and to her offspring (past or present) . . . none of these hypotheses takes into account the shock caused to the adoptee by the almost inevitable differences between the two homes, whatever form these may take, and the equally proba-ble conflict of loyalties and resentments aroused, even in cases where the contact is welcomed.

It is hard to imagine a more self-righteous, self-serving view, and its core mistake is the one that makes me feel most strongly that it is very, very clear whose story this is – the lead actor is the adoptee, and everyone else is, and must accept themselves to be, the sub-plot. Further, that a psychol-ogist should be unable to see and countenance the injustices through time done to so many natural mothers, and not to imagine that we would all benefit from the truth, for her to imagine that secrets are best taken to graves, is a part of British life which I would wish exposed to the light where it might shrivel and die.

Who pissed in my porridge, you may well ask. I feel guilty now, because I have picked a paper fight first with a priest and now with an old lady in Edna Everage spectacles. But just because they're wearing vestments or carrying a handbag cannot mean one shouldn't dare to say, Enough, you're spouting dangerous nonsense.

In more enlightened circles there are those who have defined the construct of the Adoption Triad or Triangle. The three corners of this triangle are the adoptee, the adoptive parents and the birth parents. And if one accepts this geometry, then any model of adoption that chooses to ignore one of those corners is fatally flawed. And yet doesn't this seem so unfair to the adoptive parents, who've put in so much work? The answer is – that will be up to the adoptive parents. If they consider themselves blessed to have had this child animating the middle part of their lives, they will know that fairness is not the issue and that to have worked for your children was a corrolary of loving them. But if they have come to believe, as many natural parents do too, that the child is a possession, they are mistaken, and riding for a fall. It is not possible to dominate two points in the Adoption Triangle, for it is your lot that you may only answer for one.

In 1965 the Archbishops of Canterbury, York and Wales commended 'A Service of Blessing upon the Adoption of a Child'. It has as part of its introduction the following passage:

> This service is intended to serve the needs of adopting parents who wish to recognise before God the adoption of a child into their family; and to receive within the Family of the Church God's blessing upon their

undertaking . . . The prayer for the natural parents of
the child should in no case be omitted, as full reception in Christian love must necessarily encompass all
whose lives which are met in the adoption.

The prayer for the natural parents is simple, graceful,
and placed with care after a full and deserved acknowl-
edgement that the stars of this new show are the child and
his adoptive mother and father.

We are met, first, to render thanks unto God: for the
life now gathered into your care; for the love that has
led you to afford him a welcome; and for the home
that is now both yours and his. God, in his goodness,
has thus provided for his need and for yours . . . Let
us pray . . . O God, whose property is ever to have
mercy, behold with thy love the father and mother of
this child. Keep them severally by thy grace, and lead
them in the paths of righteousness, to their own great
happiness and the blessing of all who walk with them.
May thy peace be in their hearts; through Jesus Christ
our Lord. Amen.

I have been unable to trace the committee or synod
session that originated that prayer, but I would have loved
to have been in that room and given the warmest of thanks
to each and every one of those Christian men and women.

* * *

The photographs arrived three days later. There was one of Ann and Michael sitting at their garden table together smiling into the camera. She looked pretty, suntanned, secure in her own garden. He looked like central casting trade union man from the mid-seventies – a shock of white hair, unfashionable glasses, a man who could strike a deal.

And there was the family, Maeve with long brown hair and a denim dress, Barry with a cheesy grin, Shane looking young and tall, Finian held by Michael, Liam's wife Anita holding Donnacha. And, superbly, Liam, holding a baby bottle just as if it were a bottle of Budweiser.

I don't respond well to photos, I tend not to believe them. But Lydia looked at the family photo, with a Christmas tree in the background, and was amazed. 'You look like all of them,' she said. 'You look as if you could be slipped into this photo and it would be exactly the same family, but it would make more sense.'

The problem for a person finding themselves in my position in, for example, either England or the United States is that the effect of a social policy that took the line of least resistance for fifty years – repotting children in new homes and scorching the earth in which they had grown before their birth – is that we find ourselves in my own dilemma of that momentous Sunday evening in June. What do we say to our adoptive families next? Although my personal situation was messy, and one that I did not and I believe could not deal with satisfactorily, there is an international example of the management of the adoption search that shows the way ahead for other nations.

The story of adoption in Australia runs along the same tracks as the story in England and the United States. In the nineteenth century there was no such thing as confidentiality in adoption. Children retained their original name and added the adoptive parents' name, creating an unlikely crop of Bruce Fortescue-Smythes. It was not until the 1920s that the practice of issuing a second birth certificate developed, which had the corrolative effect of denying the adoptee access to that vital first certificate, the one with the names of his mother and father.

As in the United States, secrecy was deemed to protect the child, and to an extent the adoptive parents, from the stigma of illegitimacy. For many this secrecy worked well during their childhoods, although there are many instances recorded in Australia of adoptive parents who never got round to telling their children that they even were adopted.

Australia, like the rest of the Western world, became uneasy about denying the initial birth certificates to adopted children and in the 1980s (dates vary from state to state), ten years or so after England and Wales, legislation was introduced to allow access for children over eighteen.

Thus far the model is near identical to elsewhere, a revision aimed at dealing with the inconsistency that one group of adopted children, those adopted today, were subject to the procedures of open adoption, while another group,

perhaps only ten years their senior, were subjected to locked
filing cabinets and limbo with regard to their personal birth
history. The Australians, though, have properly thought
through the implications of the idea of the Adoption
Triangle, and realised that each party – birth parents, adoptive parents and adult child – have a valid interconnection.
If one accepts this idea, which does seem to be humane and
wise, then one has to deal with the most controversial line
of connection in the Triangle – that route from birth parents
to child.

What the Australians realised was that it was not good
enough merely to broadcast heart-rending television documentaries featuring sobbing women in their fifties who had
given their children away simply because of their illegitimacy, often under duress, and knew nothing of what they
became. Nor was it satisfactory to lick the wound with the
occasional tabloid story of a long-lost child who has traced
and been joyously received by his birth mother after thirty
years, even if the article is accompanied by a photograph
of adoptive mother, birth mother and child all toasting the
camera with a glass of champagne. The Australians courageously understood that if all corners had rights then the
birth mothers had rights too.

What no adopted child wants to happen is for someone
to turn up out of the blue, a real-life version of the Michael
Brennan I dreamed about the night before he phoned. So
the Australians have opened records to all those who can
prove a connection to the Adoption Triangle, and wisely

even allowed, under the strictest of conditions, grand-parents, descendants and siblings over eighteen to obtain the release of information. They have also put in place two safeguards, which clearly protect the interests primarily of either birth mother or child: adoptees, adop-tive parents and birth parents can use an 'information veto' to prevent the release of identifying information about themselves to any of the other parties: and they may also use a 'message box' system to explain by letter to the party instigating the search precisely why they have vetoed that information.

The most immediate effect is to allow all parties to estab-lish the simple fact as to whether the others are alive or dead, which seems to be the minimum that a civilised society should be allowing a birth mother to know. A secondary effect is to permit the birth parents to be pro-active while constraining their freedom to make an unwel-come arrival. A provision allows the seeker information, with the intention of putting their minds at rest about circumstances: it would probably be accompanied by a letter explaining why the sought did not want to take things further, while preventing contact – a 'contact veto'.

There is one aspect of this system that I consider to be the wisest of all reforms. An information veto cannot be placed unless the person requesting the veto has received counselling on the effect of the veto and the possible benefits of information exchange. Once the decision is made to place the veto, it can be placed for a specific period but then perhaps reviewed and cancelled at a later stage. In the case of a contact veto having been placed, the director-general of Family and Children's Services also has the discretion to contact a person who has placed the veto to see if they still wish it to remain or be varied or cancelled.

This is the best likeness of a just legislative and practical framework I have come across. A system where the Adoption Triangle is recognised. One that enshrines the role of the adoptive parents, even if it is not the same role as the one they signed up for. One that allows the child to trace without guilt, a single stage at a time, and allows them to receive an explanation if they are still not wanted as part of their natural parents' lives, and one that gives them the option to control the stage at which they might be contacted by those natural parents, without letting them deny them the information that they are alive.

It is unsupportable, however, either that the birth mothers should be condemned to eternal unknowing, or that a generation of adoptive parents who adopted when records were closed should be condemned in any way just because open adoption is now accepted practice. In Australia the difficulty for the ranks of adoptive parents is that, while not so long ago the perception, even their self-perception, was of their rescuing, saintly role in the life of an orphan, this generalised view has mutated against them as a result of stories of babies effectively being smuggled from the Philippines or the Ukraine.

Susan Mann, a South Australian nurse, counsellor and adoptive parent has fairly sounded a note of caution:

> There are several stories running in parallel within adoption. The birth parent story, the adopted person's story and the adoptive parent story are the most obvious but by no means all. Currently certain significant aspects of the birth parent and adopted person story are taking precedence. However, adoptive parents carry with them the acute knowledge that they are parenting another's child and, in my professional experience, for the large majority of these parents their love and commitment for that child is total in its expression. The advent of open adoption in South Australia has resulted in confusion for many parents who adopted their children prior to the change in legislation in 1988. They have to reinvent their role with very little support or understanding of what that means in a current context that is questioning the validity of adoption practice. In South Australia 26,500 adoption orders were granted between 1927 and 1993. It is easy to deduce that there are over 100,000 people touched by adoption in this state alone. Adoption remains part of their future . . .
>
> I am concerned that the shame and guilt that was so much part of the birth mother's experience in earlier decades is now appearing to be transferred to adoptive parents. While acknowledging the intense

emotion that surrounds adoption I don't believe that
the answer lies in more reaction, anger or violation of
any of the parties involved.*

I do not intend to drift off into some kind of theatrical
memoir, but I should warn that I am about to use the word
Stratford-upon-Avon. It was high summer by now, and
five or six weeks after I had spoken to Ann and Michael
for the first time. Although I was eager to go to Dublin to
meet them, I was in the middle of a filming schedule at the
Royal Shakespeare Company and could not string two days
together to get away. This enforced delay gave me a period
of latency. I suspected that I needed it, because the momentum of my adoption quest was in danger of becoming a
mere blur.

One of that season's shows at the RSC was *A Midsummer
Night's Dream*, directed by the Artistic Director of the RSC,
Adrian Noble. By the interval of the opening night I was
sure it was the best *Dream* I had ever seen and that it would
be a genuine loss if it was not recorded for posterity. By the
end of the show I had realised that since I was already
filming there, if I failed to take some kind of initiative probably no recording would ever be made. So it was that that
single summer night in Warwickshire, when I was still in
the first heat of the events with Ann and Michael, led to

---

* Susan Mann, 'Adoptive Parents – A Practice Perspective'. *Adoption and
Fostering* Volume 22, Number 3, 1988.

three years' involvement in what became a film based on the production.

Producing a film is rather like being adopted – a lot of people have a fair idea of their bit of the story, but only you know the full real-life script. When the film was eventually transmitted on Channel Four on Boxing Day three years later it was magnificent, everything I could have hoped it would be and that Adrian would achieve on that summer's night. But in between, and in order to finance the project, we found ourselves led into the asylum of the 'British film industry', making a film that was never properly intended for cinema release but having to go through all the agonies of wiseacres saying, 'This doesn't look as if it was ever intended for cinema release.'

It was a fantastic paradox. There were four magical and technically first-rate leading performances from Alex Jennings, Lindsay Duncan, Desmond Barrit and Finbar Lynch, and many sublime moments where Adrian's direction, Anthony Ward's design and Howard Blake's music all soared together, yet it was judged unsuccessful for the cinema, where it was *never* meant to be shown, and then unreviewed as television, where it was *always* meant to be shown, because it did not arrive garlanded from its tiny release in the cinema. The bravehearts who cooked up the release of the film at Channel Four said, 'Never complain, never explain,' which might help illuminate how the recently predicted new dawn for British film has, yet again, spluttered out before breakfast.

But I relish the fact that the beginning of the most fertile passage in my adoption story has *A Midsummer Night's Dream* at its centre. I don't know if I'd have loved my Shakespeare as much if I'd been raised in Ireland. In France and Germany and even unexpected places such as Japan, he is accorded a paramount cultural role even though he is not one of their own. The Ireland of the time of my childhood, though, would have been a country understandably stressing the virtues of the home team, from Synge to Yeats.

It would have been a great loss to me, however, if I hadn't had my ever changing circle of Shakespearean heroes, and Bottom was my first. As an eleven-year-old I was taken from school to see a well-pitched production in the Open Air Theatre at Regent's Park. I thought the fairy stuff was unendurable, but I found my absolute hero in this crude mechanical, Bottom, who crashed on to the stage and took the piss out of its very artifice by mounting the lamentable *Pyramus and Thisbe*. His conviction that he could play Pyramus and Thisbe himself, while also playing the lion, had us all, junior cynics every one, hooting with laughter on the underground train from Great Portland Street and all the way home. What we loved was the mismatch between his self-belief and his actual ability. As an eleven-year-old you are becoming aware of the absurd egomaniac you have been for the first eleven years of your life, and realise that now is the time to look for more sophisticated ways to move about in the world.

So now here I was, in Stratford at its most bewitching, living this supreme, unlooked-for sequence of revelations at the heart of my life – and there was Bully Bottom again. Only this time I noticed that he wasn't just an ass – although he was that all right, especially in love – but he was also an enthusiast, a collaborator, a dreamer. He was not the man he thought himself to be, but he was a man who everybody loved, an unvanquished spirit. The better part of a man, I knew then, I know now, is his Bottom. 'We will meet; and there we may rehearse most obscenely and courageously. Take pains; be perfect; adieu.'

By now my story had been told so often and had travelled so fast that I found myself in the Dirty Duck pub in Stratford being told by an actress 'about this man who didn't know he was Irish and sort of traced, and anyway it was amazing' before I could tell her that I'd heard this one already.

Over the next six weeks there was an exchange of letters between Ann and me, and between Michael and me. In writing this book I have waived any claims to my own privacy in my adoption quest. I can choose how much to reveal of myself, and I have chosen not to hide anything at all – to do so would be an act of premier league hypocrisy in the context. My natural parents, however, wrote letters that they would never have dreamed might be read by any person other than myself, so it would be wrong for me to quote from them.

My impression was, however, that they were working a

variation of their normal *modus operandi*. Michael had taken a judgement and was going to back it with action – that he should do his darnedest to facilitate a meeting between us all – while Ann was more quietly considering the emotional consequences. Michael is both an instinctive player and, being a political animal, one who knows how to move the pieces about the board pretty well, especially in a crisis. Ann goes along with much of this, but she has all the authority of the Irish matriarch when she decides that part of his plan does not suit the nicer feelings of a situation.

On the phone Michael and I had established a searingly honest tone. It was very easy for me to say, 'Michael, there will be people in my situation who just want to come round and kick your fucking head in, but I am not one of them and I want you to know that,' and for him to counter, 'Well, that's just as fucking well, because Ann is a lovely woman and so are the other four kids and I wouldn't want some fucker coming over here with the intention of fucking it all up.' This was just as I would have wished it, no bullshit, both accepting that there has been some kind of balls-up, both now applying ourselves to setting it right.

Ann was more complex. I think she believed that since she had been carrying such a heavy load of guilt about what had happened for so many years I too must be carrying an equal and opposite wagonload of resentment and bitterness. She needed to proceed a little more cautiously. We got along well on the phone but in her letters she properly let her emotions show. In this I was grateful for the period of delay before the first meeting. I knew that I would be much happier to get most of the heavy-duty guilt stuff out of the way before I actually headed for Ireland. I wasn't going to be carrying absolution in my hand luggage. If you believed in a Catholic Church that planted the guilt in the first place, then that was the only place to go to shed it now that circumstances had so dramatically changed.

But I thoroughly enjoyed teasing her about that Catholicism, that every few sentences in her letters were punctuated with 'P.G.', which to me meant either Wodehouse or a nice cup of tea. (It's 'Please God', for all you heathen Henry VIII adherents.) I was also delighted, having asked her what this 'Hail Mary' thing was that I'd heard about on TV comedies, to be sent her handwritten version, together with a Virgin Mary medallion, inscribed 'For My Anglican Son, Paul'. I was thrilled to get this; I am godfather to my best friend's son and have already renounced Satan for him in a rather underqualified way at the Catholic church in Wimbledon. I felt as if I now had the proper membership card to go godfathering with some majesty.

I had flown into Dublin Airport once before, a long time ago, and when I flew back out again I had no desire ever to return.

In 1989 Lydia and I went to Dublin to cover, for various papers and magazines, the Dublin Theatre Festival. At that stage, of course, I was clueless as to my Irish marrow, and

I looked at Ireland with a naive and dispassionate eye. Unfortunately I discovered that I disliked it intensely, and was alarmed how my view of Dublin jarred with that of other people at a time when the city was just beginning to be a fashionable destination.

It began on the plane. There is no reason for air stewardesses/cabin operatives not to come in all shapes and sizes, but it seemed positively weird that our Aer Lingus cabin supervisor was both vast and aggressively in your face. No frills, just 'Put that seatbelt on' and 'We have no blankets. It'll warm up in all likelihood after take-off, and you're to know it's a very short flight.' And every time she beat a march down the aisle her oblivious buttocks would jolt the shoulders of her passengers, spilling Ballygowan water on to my trousers. I feared that on her return up the aisle she would see my wet patch and say, 'We have lavatories for that type of business.' Flights to Dublin at that time were not cheap, yet I felt like a student on a National Express coach.

For our car around Ireland I had selected the cheapest company I could find. Its premises were out somewhere near the great stadium at Lansdowne Road. I slapped down a healthy cash deposit, happily ticked boxes and signed forms and seeing that the hirer was about to give me the keys, put my hand out to receive them. To my amazement, she snatched the keys back and thrust her bunched fist beneath the counter. 'I'm to tell you that this is a new car and we don't expect it to come back damaged.'

My slow-to-rise hackles twitched a notch or two. 'You'll be waving goodbye to this deposit if it is, but we'll have the rest of it from yourself as well if the insurance doesn't cover the cost of repair.' At this moment I realised what you pay for by hiring from Budget at the airport. I dislike pompous international travellers, but I couldn't understand why as a customer I had to be told off by an air hostess and a car hire receptionist within a couple of hours, why I should be sucked into a culture where the customer was not always right but guilty, guilty as sin.

She reluctantly gave me the keys. 'Will it be all right if I switch the engine on?' I asked. Before that moment I had never appreciated exactly what a withering glance can do to a fully grown man. She watched as I reversed out into the road, and I felt as if I had walked into a situation comedy, where the next cut would have me walking back in, an hour later, with an oil-covered face, upright hair, gripping a bent steering wheel in my hands.

We were going to spend two nights in a new wing at the Jury's Hotel, Ballsbridge, but because of a cock-up at the Bord Failte (the Irish Tourist Board) our first night was spent on an arterial road leading out of Dublin in a gloomy, flock-wallpapered bed and breakfast. This again seemed designed to confound our expectations – weren't Irish land-ladies the pride of Ireland? So how come I found a full ashtray under our bed, and breakfast was served by a man with a fag in his mouth? The B&B was located in an area of Dublin I have not been able to find since, somewhere

on the road south towards Bray, but I remember the
impression that street after street seemed to have had its
upper storeys chopped off. These tiny little single-floor
houses, which I'd assumed were confined to the west,
leaked peaty smoke into the atmosphere. I am too young
to remember London smog and the chill atmosphere of
post-war rationing, but that one night made me feel as if I
had experienced it after all.

When we moved into Jury's it served only to heighten
the contrast between the modern world and what mostly
lay around us. It was quite extraordinarily luxurious, and
the service was stupendously efficient and charming. In its
main hall a huge dinner dance was being entertained by a
showband. I had never heard the term 'showband' before
this trip, and I could not believe that ten old farts in green
suits playing 'Tie A Yellow Ribbon Round The Old Oak
Tree' could be filling a venue at the heart of this modern
complex.

I feel odd about this now, slagging Dublin. It has
changed, even in ten years, almost beyond recognition. It
was stupid of us to go to a working man's pub on the south
bank of the Liffey and expect that our English accents
wouldn't attract hostile glances. But, then, why should it
be stupid? It hadn't happened in Paris or Zurich or Cologne
or anywhere I had ever been before. It was undoubtedly
stupid of me, in my silly little hired car, to flick a V sign
at a driver who cut me up, but was I even then to expect
that, in a one-way street, he would grind to a halt and begin

to reverse into me? That incident, near St Stephen's Green, had a dark, sullen, vengeful quality about it that my encounters with road rage elsewhere have wholly lacked. I felt as if I were being drawn into that final scene in *The Long Good Friday* where the IRA guys are driving Bob Hoskins to meet his maker.

And maybe we took a really unfortunate route into the countryside, but I couldn't believe the ugliness of some of the new buildings, an appalling importation of Tex-Mex architecture into an entirely unsuited landscape. Why shouldn't I have believed the hotel receptionist who said that a drive above Killiney would be like seeing the Bay of Naples? When we got there we discovered that Killiney is to the Bay of Naples what Ramsgate is to Antibes. The self-delusion rattled me.

There were just two places I saw and loved – the old monastic settlement of Glendalough in the Wicklow Mountains, and the Martello Tower at Sandycove, which is now a museum to James Joyce. I don't usually go in for this, but I prevailed upon Lydia to take a photograph of me on the rocks that Joyce had stood on himself with Sandycove in the background. I think Joyce would have understood my response to his native land, and would have appreciated that by betraying it in print, I was earning my stripes as an Irishman.

This time I was setting out for Dublin from a different point on the compass. England had changed too. The glass vastness of Stansted Airport was brand new. The arrival of the cut-price, cut-throat Ryanair was also new.

I'd had my hair cut the week before in Blackheath, and in stressing that I wanted a sort of invisible tidy-up rather than a noticeable crop I told the hairdresser why I needed to look my best. That haircut took two hours, as each emotional probe the hairdresser made was matched by just two snip-snips of her scissors. She seemed to be living the days that lay ahead for me, but she did a fine job with my hair – a haircut that didn't look like a haircut, the eternal grail for the top of my head. The hairdresser as latter-day confessor, and for her, I think, another kind of grail, a customer in her chair who has divulged more than whether he's been on his holidays.

A little part of Stansted is forever Ireland, for in a very clever retail placement the main café there is a branch of Bewley's, the popular, wood-panelled tea and coffee house chain that dominates Dublin, where it provides a friendly and attractive option to the pub as a place to meet. I began to look around for Irish faces, but the flights out of Stansted head all over Europe and it was too soon to sense an Irish contingent. I walked towards departures, pumping glucose into my blood with a kick of Cadbury's, and headed towards the gate where Flight LDW8JT would board, bound for Dublin.

And here it happened, in the seated waiting area by the departure gate, looking out at our luggage being stowed in the plane below. The internationally diverse passengers of the main airport had melted away and I stood surrounded by people who looked like me. Many of them even looked precisely like me – men of five feet, ten inches, a stone and a half over weight, with black hair, blue eyes, five o'clock shadow even at 9.45 a.m., big heads and expressions that switched from brooding to twinkling in less time than it takes to blink an eye. Their clothes were like mine, casual, clean, neutral, without show. Some smoked, some drank, but many of them, creatures of the new Eire, looked like they jogged, played football, would be good men to have by your side in the jungle. Never in my life had I felt part of an ethnic group, and I fought for a moment to resist it. Then I yielded. I knew that I wouldn't get a bollocking from the cabin supervisor this time; she was probably a distant cousin.

Beyond the ranks of himselves were our female equivalent, some of whom were young and carrying portfolios of artwork, or looked as if they did PR for a boy band. I had an unspeakably reductive thought, where I realised that if I had married one of them, rather than into the longer-limbed, smaller-browed gene pool of Lydia, my beautiful children would have grown to look, when they were old, like the snowy-haired, watery-eyed old ladies supping water in the obedient seated group led by a nun – gnomic, in both senses of the word.

Taking my seat on the plane I had that rising feeling in the stomach, the one that happens on the morning of a critical job interview. I had all sorts of things to read, from the

Rough Guide to Ireland to a volume of stories by William Trevor, *The News from Ireland*, but I couldn't swallow a single word. I was sitting next to a businesswoman in telecommunications, also the parent of two, who was on her way home from a conference. On a flight to Sydney I might have attempted to tell my story, to make myself available for a little received wisdom, but on this flight, less than an hour in the air, I couldn't even make a start. I was cross with myself. She seemed to have intuited that I was holding something back about the reason for my journey, and I felt annoyed that naturally she would have judged me as a typically reserved Englishman. What I really wanted to do was go with her and her husband for a lengthy briefing session on how to be Irish once we landed.

The English Midlands gave way to the North-West, and then we crossed the coast and over the Irish Sea. I'd read that if Sir Christopher Wren had placed St Paul's Cathedral at the deepest point of the Irish Sea, the dome I can now see from my office would still jut out of the water, glistening and barnacled. Six hundred feet deep, that was all. What loss would there be to Irishman or Brit if it were drained, I wondered, if those two sulking neighbours were bound by land as once they would have been? I made some dry-mouthed conversation, attended every word of my air hostess, who was not vast, not rude, who for every small obedience on my part said, 'Thanks a million.'

Below I saw Ireland's Eye, the island opposite the town of Howth and the first Irish soil one sees when arriving by air. Then the tower blocks north of Dublin, the legacy of the same breed of social planners who had nearly wasted my own homeland of south London. Here, seemingly in the middle of nowhere, these high-rise flats seemed so pointless – how could space be at a premium when there was so much land around them?

Fields now, a school, some suburban housing, more fields and ahead the lights of the runway. It used to happen to me with job interviews this way too, the mind blank with numbness, the deep unconscious mind preparing for fight or flight. The nose cone rose a little, the wheels glided on a few feet of air, and then touched down, with a scorching kiss, in Ireland. We cruised towards the terminal building, still at impressive speed, swung left and halted. A wheeled staircase, one that would never see the inside of a house or home, pressed against us, the cabin door was flung open, and we were released. I was very ill with pneumonia once, and I could only move at a quarter of my normal speed, no matter how hard I pressed my foot on the gas. It was like that now, all the other passengers briskly retrieving their hand luggage from above, scrumming down gently to push themselves through the open door. I followed them, detached, floating. 'Thanks a million,' said the stewardess.

The arrivals area was new, not at all as it had been before. I passed by a well-lit counter selling croissants and cappuccino and walked into a sea of the same people I had mingled with at Stansted. We were everywhere. There was no need for me to reclaim my luggage – it was all in a black bag I had with me on the plane. God, I thought, I wish I did have to reclaim some luggage, buy myself a little time before I press on. I've seen that Algerian man at Orly Airport in Paris, who became resident on a bench in a dispute over his visa, for more than a decade, and I felt I needed at least a week on a Dublin Airport bench to still my beating heart. I looked behind me, and saw that a retreat to clamber back on the plane was impossible. Ahead of me was a long straight walk to arrivals. I grabbed a trolley, slung my baggage aboard, and pushed it as slowly as was possible without actually coming to a halt.

Nothing to declare through customs, turning right now, and seeing to the left the automatic sliding doors that would carry me out of arrivals and into the open airport concourse. Someone twenty yards ahead of me passed through, and I saw the eager faces of the friends, relatives and drivers of a hundred other passengers, all hoping that the next one through was theirs.

My forward motion now ceased entirely. I thought of the other times in my life when I'd summoned the courage to walk over a cliff. In truth, not many. Perhaps I had become adept at avoiding moments such as this. Maybe part of maturity was to accept that on occasion there is a role to be played and the world expects one to play it to the full, although coming out of arrivals is the opposite of going on stage, because you can be sure that nearly everybody there is looking not at you, but past you. But two pairs of eyes were focused on me. Michael was the first forward, a huge smile and a massive hug. 'Welcome home, son,' he said. Not home, I thought, but what else could he say? Typically, it was the most generous and effusive remark available to him. He looked ten years younger than his photograph. His hair may have been snowy white but it positively burst through his scalp. His skin was unlined and glowing.

'Now, I said to you on the phone that I didn't know if Ann would be able for it, but here she is,' he announced. I looked beyond another family reunion and there was Ann, twenty years younger than her photograph, eyes brimming, probably terrified, wearing a smile of complete and utter love. We too hugged, and kissed. I stood back from them both.

'You look a lot younger than your photographs.'

'Well, that's because this is a special day to have you back,' said Michael. I smiled. 'Let's get out of here,' he continued. 'I have the car across the way.'

Ann put her arm through mine and we passed back out into the Irish air, which, even with aviation fuel hanging in the atmosphere, smelled about a quarter as polluted as that of south-east London. This moment had become one of the most significant of my life, although even then I knew that my marriage and the birth of my children would always be more important. This was fine, but I was fearful that it might not be enough for these new natural parents.

For what they had become in that meeting were the best aunt and uncle ever in the world, and at first this was the best that could be expected. It would have been impossible in that instant – or it would have been for me – to have thrown myself at their necks sobbing, 'Mummy, Daddy.' When I looked at Ann and Michael I saw two individuals who, when they had their crisis pregnancy, were a great deal younger than I was then, standing before them at Dublin Airport. In Ann's case, more than a decade younger. For the people they had been in 1961 I felt nothing but enormous, genuine sympathy, as I would do today if I came across a woman in her twenties who found herself in such a complete mess. I felt, I suppose, like my own parents' kindly uncle.

I'm told that there is often a moment in a parent's later life where their grown-up child becomes in a practical sense like a parent to them. I seemed to have skipped straight to the beginning of that phase without anything that had gone before, but in truth this is the only way I would have wanted it. From my love for Jake and Benjamin I could imagine the emotions that must be coursing through this married couple, these parents of four, these losers of their first-born, now returned. What lay ahead of me now was the most difficult journey of all, to see whether I had enough love in me to return.

As it happened, there was a much more difficult journey instantly to be undertaken.

Throughout the 1980s and on into the 1990s, privatisation of state-owned industries had swept irresistibly across the United Kingdom. Ireland was no longer immune, and the Irish government was desperate to do something about the financial black hole of the state airline, Aer Lingus. Of all the privatisations in smaller countries, the state airline is always one of the most contested, for an airline flies that country's flag around the globe, shows the international community that it has the wherewithal to borrow a ton of money for two more transcontinental aeroplanes. In Ireland this debate was as heated as anywhere else, and the government had attempted a first-stage privatisation – of the maintenance division of the airline, Team Aer Lingus.

Michael's union represented hundreds of Team Aer Lingus workers. On the day I arrived Team Aer Lingus were on strike and attempting to close down the airport. In coming into the airport to meet his son for the first time, Michael was busting his own picket line.

'Now,' said Michael, as he scampered away down the road to an official-looking parking space he seemed confidently to have appropriated, 'there's a bit of a funny situation here with you today. I shouldn't really be here at all.' He explained the dispute. 'Now I've addressed the meeting, and if you ask me there's a few fucking headers who are going to mess it up for the rest.' The fear of the Team Aer Lingus workers was that by being privatised they were effectively giving up jobs for life for the short-term-contract ulcer we all know and love today. Michael believed he and the other union negotiators had wrangled as positive a deal as they could ever get from the management, but there was a time limit on the offer. If a full-scale strike became something that grounded the Aer Lingus fleet, humiliating the government, that good deal might be lost.

And so it was that the three of us swiftly bundled into the car with what more delicate souls might have considered undue haste in the circumstances. I have a weak spot for car comedy, and nothing can reduce me to hysteria quicker than a well-shot driving test disaster routine. I was now in a car comedy, at what was meant to have been one of the most poignant moments of my entire life. Michael reversed out hastily.

'Be careful now, Michael,' said Ann from the back seat.

'That's as well, Ann, but there's a march load of these people and it would be a fucking disaster if they see me driving an Englishman out of the airport.'

'Michael!' admonished Ann.

'I'm telling it like it is, Ann.' He turned to me. 'Ah sure, we'll be all right. I know a way out by the perimeter, and they're all coming in the other way. I saw them on the way in, placards and banners the lot.'

He shot away down the road, away from the main flow of traffic and out towards what seemed an inevitable collision with a jumbo preparing for take-off. But the road veered to the left, past high, steel fencing on the right. It felt like a road that only security vehicles and fuel tankers were allowed to take. Michael came to a T-junction ahead. 'Jeez, what do I do here? I think it's a left.' He turned right, along another road, and towards a roundabout two hundred yards further on.

Also heading towards the roundabout, which seemed to be in the middle of nowhere, miles from the nearest settlement, was a march of about a thousand unhappy men coming in from another direction. Just as Michael had said, their placards were many and vociferous. 'Oh. Oh no,' said Michael. There was no turning back. 'Maybe if I just beat them to the roundabout I'll get away without them seeing me.'

'Won't they know the car, Michael?' said Ann.

'Just keep your head down in the back there, Ann,' he replied. He pressed his foot down on the accelerator as we steamed on.

To the marchers, of course, approaching the roundabout on this godforsaken plateau, the sight of a red car accelerating towards them must have aroused mixed feelings. Undaunted by the spectre of Michael's car, their throbbing feet also gathered speed. As a group they had a collective cartoon bubble: 'We'll get to the roundabout before that fecker.'

It would have been possible for Michael to maintain his speed and get across the roundabout before the main march, but he would have had to plough through the first fifty men to do so. With thirty yards to go, his options were down to one. He slammed hard on his brakes and skidded, with some control, to a perfect halt, about six feet short of the marchers, who were now snaking around the roundabout.

'All right, we'll wait here for a moment,' he said. He might have drawn more attention to himself, I suppose, if he'd been on fire, but short of this in this empty place he was, to every man jack of the marchers, the exclusive focus of their notice. One or two of them, in a moderately stroppy fashion, semi-veered so that they could brush his front bumper with their trouser legs as they were passing. Recognition was just a matter of time.

'Jesus, Michael. Is that you in the car?'

The windows were all tightly wound up, so Michael was free just to gesticulate in a positive sort of way, while saying 'All right there, lads. Well done, there. On you go. On you go.' Helpfully he was pointing out to any doubters that they should carry on around the roundabout in a clockwise direction.

As for me, well, this trip, this first trip, was meant to have been the most secret event to have been executed in Ireland in many years. As the marchers passed, all wondering why their leader was driving in a car in the opposite direction, they took a good look at his front-seat passenger. I wondered if it would be helpful for me to duck under the windscreen, but decided that all I could do was hold my ground. As they passed by in their hundreds, Michael was smiling at them all in a thumbs-up kind of way, so I thought I'd go for the same. 'Carry on there, lads,' I projected through my smile. I looked to my right, and there he was, my father. Like the men in the photographs in the *Irish News*, like me, when he smiled it was the least sardonic smile man can make. It was a ball, a focus-busting gurn. It was one of the many things that were me that were also him.

After a few minutes our way was clear.

'Do you think they saw you, Michael?' said Ann.

'One or two of the lads. They'll have assumed I was on important business. Well, so I fucking am.'

As we pulled away Ann looked down at my hands. 'Don't you have the same hands as Michael, Paul. Not made for work.'

'He's a quality man, Ann, like myself.'

'Dead right,' I said.

6

Beneath the Field

FOR THIS most propitious of journeys to Ireland I had
planned to stay in as luxurious a hotel as I could find. I
didn't want a mere room: I wanted a pillowy boudoir, with
another room that was the complete office, and a bathroom
with jacuzzi, bidet, and foaming shower. But the Dublin
of today is no longer a destination to be taken for granted.
All the swanky hotels were completely full. The only place
I could book from London was the Doyle Tara Hotel on
the Merrion Road running south of Dublin towards Dun
Laoghaire. It was comfortable enough, but not by any
means a swank-hole. It was by the sea, though, and when
I entered my room and saw the Irish Sea I was grateful that
central Dublin had been fully booked. For what I would
need was air and light and sea, and the shifting perspective they each gave.

It is a coincidence, and not a happy one, that both Dublin

and London have such a messed-up relationship with their own rivers. Both have been steeply banked, both have thunderous traffic along those banks, neither gives the merest hint as to why anybody might have considered this a good place to build a town. And although Dublin is much nearer the sea than London, it too feels a hundred miles from it. Yet both cities are there only because of their rivers and their proximity to estuarine mouths. If you come to London and stay off Oxford Street, you might never understand this, and if I had ended up back at Jury's at Ballsbridge my room would have had no hint of why it was there at all. I am deeply susceptible to the influence of rivers and the sea, and I am equally miserable when I feel that they are not near, that all there is is the dry land beneath my feet. In the course of the events of the weekend I knew I would be able to look at this view and clear my mind, like a child shaking his Etch-A-Sketch, yielding a clean, blank slate for each new idea as it arose.

Ann and Michael would be knocking on my door in a few minutes. They had also booked into the Doyle Tara for the weekend. The secret that they had exclusively shared back in 1961 was still theirs alone. They would have loved to have invited me back to their house in Palmerstown, a western suburb of Dublin, but the questions from family and neighbours would have been pretty hard to answer. The three of us in one hotel was rather like a peace negotiation with a Monday deadline held in a secret house near Oslo. All of us were free of our daily routines and bonds, and of the telephone. All three of us were simply ourselves. The success or failure of what lay ahead would be entirely of our own making.

I unpacked my stuff and was in the middle of changing my trousers when Ann and Michael knocked at the door. At home I jettison my trousers the moment I walk in. The reason for this is practical – usually I am covered with children within seconds, and usually they are covered in fromage frais. This often creates suspicious-looking stains on my chinos, which cannot stand the strain of a daily wash at forty degrees. Our neighbours are used to the man in the boxer shorts rolling the wheelie bin up the garden path, and our postman now expresses surprise if he catches me with my trousers on. So at the Doyle Tara I opened the door trouserless.

'Look at that, Michael. Doesn't he have the same legs as Barry?'

'That'd be right, Ann.'

Like Adam realising in Eden that he hasn't got his kit on, I nipped into the bathroom and put on some clean trousers. I'd had to leave home just after six that morning, so I needed to shave as well. The room had three chairs, which I'd arranged by the window in what I realised was a slightly confrontational way – them on one side of a little table, me like an interviewee on the other, able to see them and the sea. I filled the half-sized kettle with water and put it on to boil. I asked them to make themselves comfortable and began to shave. I always wet shave and it always takes three minutes and thirty seconds. I always do something else at the same time but before now I had never realised it.

'Listen to that, Michael, he's a Brennan in the bathroom.'

'Ah we all like a good whistle, Ann.'

I dried my face and left the bathroom just as the little kettle had come to the boil. Michael, ever practical, seized the implication of the moment and went back to their room to fetch a third cup. It was then that I was left alone for the first time ever with the woman who had conceived me and given birth. She came over and gave me a huge hug, a little tearfully. 'Can you forgive me?' she said. I replied that I could forgive her anything so long as she stopped asking me about it every time we spoke. In that moment I could sense that in time she would begin to feel like a mother (though not to the exclusion of the one I already had), but also in that moment I felt odd – essentially, that I was in what probably looked like a passionate embrace with another bloke's wife. I think I'm pretty unscrewed up about expressing physical affection, but I'm not especially at ease with clinches with grown-ups who aren't my wife. It's not a significant thing really. Neither can I stand the habit in the last few years of men who come to dinner wanting to kiss me when they leave. Men's stubble – yuck.

'I'll stick a couple of teabags in,' I said, releasing myself from the embrace. Ann asked me to let her do it, but I said it was okay, London New Man knows how to do these things for himself. Just then Michael knocked at the door again. As I went to open the door, I glanced at Ann. These few moments alone hadn't been nearly enough for her. While I was coming to the beginning of the end of my journey, she was just starting hers.

I realised that my journey was the easy one, for I had no memory of the events of thirty years ago. Everything that had happened to me, from my childhood to the fruition of this search, had evolved in a slow and manageable way. For Ann, the experience had been of two heart-rending events thirty years apart. First, the birth, loss and return to Ireland, needing to obliterate the memory. And second, the baby's return, hairy and animate in front of her, with an English accent and the inevitable consequence for her of being heart-broken at what she had missed in the years in between.

We sat. 'You make a good cup of tea,' said Ann.

'Don't think much of the milk they give you in these places, though,' added Michael. Ann sighed. 'Well, I'll say this,' he went on, 'of all of them you're by far the fattest.'

'Michael!'

I laughed. 'Well, if I get to meet the others I can be like a warning from the future. I've put a stone on for each child. Lydia did too, but she lost it every time she gave birth. Don't worry, it's not beer, it's chocolate mostly.'

'Isn't that an amazing thing though altogether, Ann? Your sister, Maeve, she'd be mad for the chocolate.'

'Oh she's dreadful, isn't she Michael? You know some-times she hides the wrappers and you find them in the most peculiar places. Do you not take a drink though, Paul?'

I said that half a pint of beer was usually too much for me. Michael's eyes lit up.

'Aren't I the same, Ann? I never liked the taste.'

'He likes the chocolate though, Paul. Oh, he's a pig once he's got the box open.'

'A tin, Ann, that's what I like. Do you have those big round tins in England, Paul?'

'What, like Quality Street?'

'And that Cadbury's Roses. Ah, marvellous stuff.'

'I get the tin out when we've company,' said Ann, 'and, Paul, doesn't it always end up by the side of his chair, with his great hand dipping in and out. I'm sure he doesn't bother taking the wrapper off sometimes.'

'That'd be the best bit, Ann.'

'I came down one night, he'd fallen asleep with his hand in the tin.'

Michael had used the few moments of banter to formulate an answer to my earlier implied question. 'You'll meet the others right enough. We had to meet you first, I'm sure you can understand that, but as I said I know you're a good man. It'll be difficult for us, but as soon as this weekend is over we'll tell them.'

And we chatted on for an hour or so more, until eventually it was time to eat some lunch. I'd already said that I'd been to Dublin once before and had been photographed by the Martello Tower at Sandycove. Michael said that it was still a grand place, and the weather was beautiful, so why didn't we head down in that direction and see what we could find to eat. When we got there there were no cafés or restaurants open, and the local shops didn't inspire. But there was a fish and chip shop – a chipper.

And so, at about half past one on 23 July, I sat on the seafront at Sandycove, the Martello Tower in the distance to our right, and I ate fried fish, which I normally loathe, and chips with curry sauce, which I had never had. Thank God I wasn't brought up here, I thought. If I'd discovered chips and curry sauce earlier in my life I'd be too fat to move. And sitting either side of me, as I dipped the chips into the polystyrene pot, were my natural parents, who I had never met before. I love the sound of seagulls, and that day they were playing a symphony. And I love the smell of the sea, and that day its warm breeze smelled like the beginning of life itself.

Imagine living your entire childhood in a country village, in Dorset say, with a bedroom that had a view over a large, undulating field, and that as a child you'd accepted the field simply as a walled pasture, with odd little hillocks upon which to play King of the Castle.

Imagine, then, reaching the beginning of the age of curiosity and analysis, and discovering that there were such things as Ordnance Survey maps. You find and study the map for your own village and discover the different altitudes running from one side of the field to the other, and perhaps you make a flattering comparison between yourself as the player on the hillocks and the new you who can read and analyse maps, who can explain to yourself why your favourite field has the multi-levelled character you have unconsciously loved all this time.

Imagine further. You look through your window one day and a local historian in an anorak is treading about in your field. You are the expert. You rush outside and challenge him, brandishing your Ordnance Survey Map to indicate your authority. He takes it from your hand, lays it on the flat top of a tree trunk, and from his satchel withdraws a plastic transparency. He lays it precisely on top of your OS map and shows you the highly detailed, black outline of an ancient priory that once stood in the field, entirely unbeknownst to you. You are taken aback, suspicious at first, but he patiently shows you that his transparency fits your many-levelled field to the inch. He demonstrates how your favourite ridge is perfectly explained by the subterranean presence of the refectory steps, covered in soil for hundreds of years. He shows you how you can relate every single inch of this favourite childhood playground to his enlightening transparency.

Perhaps you don't like surprise: you are angry that the whole of the fabric of your childhood is challenged by this. But the historian tells you not to fear, he comes across this every day. The field and its undulating top soil are unchanged by his transparency, and so is your childhood. He just thought you would like to know what was underneath. You hesitate. You ask if he is going to want to dig it up. He says that he isn't, because although it's a surprise

to you, these old buried priories are everywhere. He will
do some sonar scans to prove what he has discovered, but
it's too late to change the field now. He did think, though,
that your children might be excited to know what really lay
beneath their feet.

Ireland is not, and never has been, about chips with curry
sauce. I am keen not to make unfounded claims for my new
old country, but I will make one. Ireland's actors and writers
use the language of English better than the people of any
other country in the world. I spent my twenties going to
farflung parts to review plays that threw up dozens of
examples of this in unlikely locations, from campaigning
plays seeking the release of the Birmingham Six to the ever
diverse canon of Spike Milligan, who I am proud to declare
is not only Irish and hung up on India, as am I, but spent
the most miserable years of his life in Lewisham – our own
local anti-hero.

So it was a brilliant and generous stroke for Ann and
Michael to have booked tickets for the Gaiety Theatre for
that night, to see a revival of a world-famous adaptation of
Brendan Behan's *Borstal Boy*. The production's energy shot
out from under the proscenium arch, the ensemble talent
terrifying when compared to what one might expect from
a similar production in London. It was also riveting, for
Behan was writing freely about the IRA years before the
Troubles reignited in 1969, so he was able to say not only
how there was something in their cause, but also that it

attracted some of Ireland's prizest arseholes. The audience at the Gaiety hooted with laughter at all this, and adored every moment of lampooning at the expense of authority figures, and, in particular, the hairy-eared priest. Perhaps the theatre has been the one place in Ireland that has regularly had the courage to say up yours to the established Catholic Church: it does so with almost indecent relish.

Michael had been on stage from the airport to the collection of the theatre tickets, so he managed to snatch a pretty deep sleep during the second half. Ann seemed determined to stay alert and make sure that I was enjoying it, which I was, and, after an initial shriek, she coped well with the moment when twelve borstal boys pulled down their trousers and flourished their genitalia to the audience. I was delighted by this. When I was born it was as unthinkable that this could happen on an Irish stage as that Ann could give birth after a four-month pregnancy. Now the enormous fruit of that pregnancy could return to Ireland free of shame, and young men on stage could air their undercarriages, and nobody could do a thing to stop us.

The thing about the next morning, Sunday, is that I just don't get enough church in my life. I've already confessed to Westminster Cathedral, but for years I also went to St Lawrence Jewry Church by the Guildhall in the City of London, every Tuesday lunchtime, where they hold boneshaking organ recitals. I've done synagogue, Hindu temple, outdoor Buddhism, and some impressive, total immersion baptisms. And Exeter Cathedral – I must have walked so much misery around that beautiful place that I'm sure I've left faint black stains under some of the arches. With the arrival of children, however, time spent in church is nappies unchanged and food uncooked. I'd retreated to the ranks of those who shoot up on god by smelling their children's temples, or by standing like an oak tree in their darkened bedroom, breathing their sleep.

I do believe in god, and I'm certain what it is. There is no afterlife. Heaven and hell are here on earth, and contemplation, meditation or prayer will reveal whether something you're about to do will walk you up a righteous path or send you down a sulphurous alley. You'll be judged by your friends, your lovers, your kids and, in the last trump, by yourself. You're not coming back, but in what you've left behind you do live on. If in doubt, Sermon on the Mount. You can do great work inspired by the spirit of god, but if you invent a uniform for god and do work in god's name it will always fall off the rails. By working in god's army you identify the godless, enmity follows and the rest is history.

So I'm not orthodox anything, but I love those churches, those ceremonies, even when they're boring. Even a bad sermon illuminates the beauty of the good sermon the vicar would have given if he hadn't been worrying about the church roof. So when Ann and Michael asked what I wanted to do that Sunday morning I said, 'Take me to church.'

The Whitefriars Church in Aungier Street is almost next door to Michael's union headquarters on the south side of

the Liffey. Its entrance promises very little, its frontage to
the street very narrow. But, like Dr Who's Tardis, once
inside it immediately bursts into an enormous space that
would do credit to a small Anglican cathedral.

The Irish at the theatre have a quite incredible habit.
While English audiences will actually wet themselves
rather than going to the loo in mid-scene, an Irish person,
remembering that he hasn't paid for his parking space, will
leap up and clamber to the aisle even if the actor has just
set off on 'to be or not to be'. An Irish church contrasts in
exactly the same way. There is a constant sense of movement and flow, of people in side chapels muttering prayer
while the priest is whispering into his microphone. Every
now and then you actually hear someone saying, 'Hello,
Deidre, how you keeping?' even as the priest is incanting
about Calvary. Once, in a different Dublin church, I was
praying quietly and a woman came up beside me and asked,
'Could you give me five pounds for to buy some potatoes.'
On her part this was probably a cunning move, for if a real
God had been listening in at the time it could have looked
bad for me to tell her to sod off. I bunged her 50p, thinking that for five pounds you could potato a rugby team.

Over the last year Ann and Michael had obviously lit a
lot of candles and sent up a lot of prayers for Maeve to recover
from illness, many of them in this church. I was moved to
see their devotion to prayer, their candle-lighting, and felt
as if I was being allowed to see them at their most intimate,
with their god. I had no beef with the Catholic Church over

adoption – the Church of England had been just as judgemental over illegitimacy – but I had equivocal feelings
about seeing them subscribe to it seemingly without reser-
vation or criticism. I love all churches, but I knew that I
only had to walk a few yards within this one to encounter
someone who would still see the Illegitimate as one of the
lower ranks of the Damned, and the parents of the
Illegitimate as lusty beasts who had no proper part in God's
creation. To see my natural parents still part of the fabric
of the church, I wondered if they had learned. If they went
back in the Tardis, would they fight not to do it all the same
again?

But Ireland, no matter how much it enters the modern
world, is a different case. As we came out of the church the
entrance was swarming with those who seemed materially
desperate, and their pleas for help, here in church, were
actually heeded. Even today if you stand at the junction of
O'Connell Street as it meets the Liffey Quay you will see
in fifteen minutes more physically disabled persons than
anywhere else in northern Europe. In Ireland, still, there
are many who see in their everyday lives that they are but
a few steps up from hell on earth, and they pray like mad
to keep from descending.

After church – opposite which is the kind of multi-jarred
sweet shop that has all but disappeared from London but
that before puberty was the focus of all my desire – we went
to Michael's union office. I've spoken to a lot of people
about him now, and they all agree that he has given every

ounce of his energy to attempt to improve the conditions of his members. In Ireland, where personal connections are still key, he has listened to and helped direct thousands of struggling men in the right direction. A few years before I met him he missed by a whisker being elected as a Labour Party Member of the European Parliament. Irish politics is still dominated by two parties that confusingly take their origins from the Irish Civil War, Fianna Fail and Fianna Gael. To get elected Labour Party anything has always been very difficult, perhaps because you're representing neither land nor town but an ideal.

We sauntered upstairs, and I saw his desk, with an epic list of handwritten tasks, one to thirty, which he would have to address on Monday, and which if I hadn't been there he would have started to address now. Ann at last had her moment, and went to make us all a cup of tea in the kitchen, while I had a good nose around the premises, which had the appearance of a modern, tightly run, union operation. I was impressed. Once again, my mind spun as I stood alone in an empty meeting room and looked out of a window to Aungier Street below.

It was all becoming so concrete, the abstract was beginning to fade away forever. My natural mother was making me a cup of tea in my natural father's office. Two months before I had not known if they were alive, and if they had been my expectations of them had been of the lowest kind, yet downstairs from me now was the leader of an Irish trade union and a woman who was clearly a much loved mother, smart, attractive, devout. Knowing this, in concrete terms, I could imagine how depressing it would have been if they had been dead, or worthless, or feckless, or wicked. I always felt I was ready for it if they had been, but now that they'd proved to be the opposite of my worst fears I wondered if I truly had.

I didn't feel that I should give thanks to a large man in the sky for all this, neither did I think that incredible forces of fate had been at work. What I saw was a thirty-two-year twist in some of the arteries of the three of us – natural mother, natural father and natural son. I was now reaping as I had sown. As I sat at the head of this committee room table, my hands resting on a blotter, I felt like a minor ancient hero who, for some small courage, has been given a golden key.

On the plane returning to my wife and two boys, I realised that there was one thing I had not found out that weekend, something that I think I shall never really know. Why did they give that baby away? What were the pressures on them, really? Did they fear their families, their church? Were they in debt? Did they . . . Does it matter? Yet we'd talked about this at length, they didn't try to conceal anything, answering questions that perhaps even I did not have a right to ask. But, in the end, this was something they had not mentioned to each other since the day I was born. Not only had they not discussed it with family or friends, they had never even discussed it between themselves. It would take the powers of a hundred anorak-wearing historians and a legion of psychologists to regress them back to the people they were back then and to give me a whole answer. Maybe that's why this question had never mattered to me: I had worked out for myself that it was a question to which there was never going to be a full answer.

I have looked but been unable to find an Irish couple of the same age who kept their child in identical circumstances, although there must have been hundreds, but it is impossible to judge or assess the actions of people so long ago by the values we hold today. In 1961 they probably both realised that they were in it up to their necks, and they took the way out that they had been told by friends. Would I have made the same decision today? No, I would have fought an army to keep our child. But then I'm in England with the right accent, a small amount of money, work, no prejudice against me, no religious conditioning, no shame, little fear. The years of my childhood, the sixties and seventies, were years when nearly every sacred cow was burned in public. To conform, to adhere was to be blind, to be paralysed. I would have fought for my child not just because I knew I would love it but because I believed in my right, my freedom, to keep it. In 1961, those who were told their child was illegitimate often believed they were bad, had done wrong, didn't deserve to defy society's judgemental stare. I don't know if any of those who would have represented the wide body of those opposed to illegitimate birth will read this book, but if you do, sleep easy.

Yes, you twisted our arteries for thirty years, but we prevailed. We beat you, and now we know who and what you are, and the madness that you preach, we will never in these two countries let you rise again.

On the train from Stansted to Liverpool Street I slumped back, exhausted. I'd slept very little that weekend and in truth I'd slept very little since Jake had been born. I'd aged and I knew it. For two of the previous four years I'd been at ITN producing overnight for Channel Four's morning arts show, and when I'd come home to sleep Jake was waking up. The bloom of youth and of my twenties had gone, and I wondered if Ann, with a mother's eye, had seen that and been concerned. Because when a child is yours it is, in aspects, also you.

My eyes and hair colour I had realised that weekend came from Ann, as did the turn of speed I'd always had on the running track. And it was in remembering that turn of speed, the source of which I had met for the first time, that I experienced my first pang of regret, the first and not last sense of a life not led, of an opportunity lost. As a teenager I'd represented south London at 400 metres, which is a lung-busting but, when you fly round those bends, thrilling event. But the population of south London is the same as the whole of Ireland. What would have happened to me in Palmerstown? Would I have gone on to represent my country, coming last in race meetings around the world? I would never know.

But these dreams of a past that had never happened were

nothing to what lay ahead nine months later, when Lydia gave birth to twin daughters, Sasha and Tara. And Tara had the hair and the eyes (and the speed, it emerged) of her grandmother, and I would have the experience of putting a little part of my own mother to bed every night.

Liverpool Street Station, like Ireland, had shed its dirty old skin over the previous decade. Leaving for Stansted at dawn the day before I had not had time to notice this, but now in this early summer's evening it was the point of my return to my home city. I was even more tired now, and I wandered weakly towards the Circle line for Embankment, then Charing Cross and home. The Circle line runs along some of the shallowest and oldest tunnels on the London Underground and, unlike the spartan functionality of other lines, it has exposed brick arches, the occasional high ceiling, wrought iron. It is very easy to imagine it when it was first built, and in my inner eye I often conjure images of Victorian men constructing it and travelling on it. Tonight I could imagine, with a chill, the orphans of a century ago who would have known it, sheltered within it, been turfed out from its sanctuary.

Those children would have to wait another thirty years before the modern era of adoption began. No wonder society wanted to hide their original birth certificates and give them a clean start. For society wasn't just ashamed of illegitimacy; it was ashamed by its own brutality in its very recent history. It too needed a clean start, and to have a collective belief in the restarting of social history. With the children's birth records wiped, we would all be absolved of the stench of cruelty and betrayal. What would I have advocated if I had been an Edwardian reformer? With what I know now I would have urged openness, but the man I would have been before would have urged that the little ones be given a new start, their shackles to the sordid past, our sordid past, cut with total force.

I reached Embankment and walked up Villiers Street to the overground station at Charing Cross, seeing many young loving couples of a warm summer's evening. When you're alone and not in love this can be a desperate sight. When you're married with two wonderful boys it astonishes you – that many of these couples will in five years' time have made the most significant rite of passage of them all, from being me, to being us, to being us and him or her. As they kissed, or bickered, or rested on each other's shoulders, I passed through them, the salt air and incense still in my hair, and wondered how many of them would use the freedom they had and still make a pig's ear of bearing a child? I felt like a grandad to everybody, including both sets of my own parents. The journey I had made was beyond any of their own experience, and I was destined to have to listen patiently to them all as they shared their fears and feelings about me.

I could cope with this, I knew, but that night there was something about which I felt profoundly unsure. To express it fully would be to invent a new, modern myth.

Oedipus cannot help, neither can Pandora. What concerned me was that I had led a life across thirty years with this neglected mystery close to the core of my being. Now I had by my own free will summoned it to the surface, and solved it, but what would fill the hole where that mystery had been? What would drive that part of the core? Where there had been doubt and unknowing and forward momentum driven by it, now there was certainty and revelation – but would there be inertia? I reasoned that surely this knowledge must be a good thing, but my heart still fluttered. The years of conditioned repression could not be shaken away in one weekend in Dublin. I sought a parallel in any story telling of 'The Man Who Solved Himself', but it didn't seem to have been told.

By the time I had walked up the garden path and breathed the scent of the prolific, almost wild English roses, Jake, who had been asleep for three hours, had decided it was morning, and I walked in the door to have him instantly placed on my shoulder. I told Lydia all I could, before she went to bed exhausted. Jake wanted to know more, and so I did the best I could to explain to this wise four-year-old the concept of Anglo-Irish relations, from the Potato Famine to Gerry Adams. Very soon, like two sozzled oldsters on a park bench, we were both unconscious on the sofa.

7

The Four-Panelled Mirror

I NEED not have feared, for while my batteries were unconsciously adapting to draw power from a new source, the tide of events would make sure that I would have sufficient momentum to carry me forward. My journey thus far I had been able to imagine to an extent, even upstairs in my office at Jake's third birthday party, but I could never have imagined that the morning after I'd returned to London Ann would phone from Dublin, the bit firmly between her teeth, a real human becoming pro-active in my own cause, an ally.

'I just want to tell you that we've had the best weekend of our lives,' she said. 'Your coming back to us has filled a terrible hole that I have tried to ignore for all these years. So I've decided, and I'll have to pick my time for this, I'm going to begin to tell your brothers and Maeve all about you.'

'God, are you sure?' I said, my feet only just touching earth from the weekend.

'We won't live a lie any more. You have a right for them to know all about you, and they have a right to know they have an elder brother.'

'Well, look, er . . .' This was unknown country. My original mission was thought through – telling a natural mother of the welfare of her child. I was not at all sure that I wanted to be involved in the destruction of the dynamics of an entire family by forcing each child to realise that, for example, he wasn't the third child, but the fourth, or that for the entire period of their childhood and adolescence their parents' minds had been, in some small part, elsewhere.

This was a section of the journey that I had never considered. Meeting two Irish parents was one thing, astonishing in itself, but not off the scale. Because they had both lived in England, even if it was at a time of No Dogs, No Blacks, No Irish in landlords' windows, and because they had deposited me when they were in Blackheath, almost in my own garden, I had accorded them a status similar to my own. English and Irish, or in their case Irish and English. But these four siblings had spent their whole lives in Ireland. Each of their individual existences would underline the inevitable differences between us. Most of all, I suppose I feared that some of them might have my own faults, and that I would see myself in a hideous four-panelled mirror, where what I thought were virtues suddenly appeared as terrible family vices, and where the vices I knew I had leered back at me in quadruple.

Ann set about her task, with conviction and courage. Liam, Maeve, Barry and Shane were to be told, in no specific order, but essentially when they were in the house or at close hand.

Maeve was first, on the Tuesday after I got home. I now know the kitchen and green-grassed garden where Ann composed herself and then told her only daughter that she had not one older brother but two. I don't know how to write this without seeming boastful, but I understand from both of them that their first reading was that I was an angel sent from heaven, despatched partly, I think, to reward them for their fortitude during Maeve's illness. Today, if they ever do think of me as an angel I am sure it is as one of the fallen kind, but it's lovely to know that it is possible to have such an effect on the lives of strangers. I'm not cut out to be Cliff Richard or Daniel O'Donnell, but on this one day I affected the sentiments of warm-hearted ladies just as that androgynous pair do with every appearance on television.

I don't know what would have happened next in England, John Major's England. Maeve would probably have consulted a family solicitor with regard to the position on inheritance before sending me a tightly worded postcard inviting me to visit if ever I was in the area (the lawyer would have been in the background, behind a rubber plant). Maeve, though, named after the Queen of

Connaught, which I had thought was a hotel off Kingsway until this wondrous Tuesday evening, went straight to the phone in her mother's house and welcomed me to the family.

Her voice over the phone was nothing like I had expected, which once again had been some cliché of Irishness. It was warm, genuine, filled with laughter, mild in tone, subversive, and sympathetic. It was my sister's voice. I had a sister, a beautiful sister, who could speak French and German, and had survived a car crash and an illness, and had a boyfriend called Lar (Lawrence) who ran a commercial refrigeration company with his dad. And if either the car crash or the illness had got her I would never have heard her voice, only seen her photographs.

Ann was wasting no time. Shane was then only twenty-one, running the world headquarters of Eagle Video (now trading as Moondance Productions, by the way) in Ann and Michael's front room. When he was not formulating the future of Irish broadcasting at the table he was in the kitchen making sandwiches – not doorsteps but whole staircases. Six feet, four inches on the hoof take a lot of refuelling, and the family fridge was Shane's pitstop every two to three hours. On one of these trips, as he teased the plastic wrap from a pair of cheese slices, Ann asked him to sit down at the kitchen table. She had something very important to discuss.

As he rested his large frame on a small chair, his arms on the table, she emphasised the importance of the moment by slapping a foolscap, brown envelope, full of documents and photographs about me, on to the table in front of her. I am told their dialogue went something like this:

'Shane, I have to tell you something very, very important.'

'Sure, go on there, Ma.'

'No, this is very serious. There is something that your daddy and I have had to keep a secret for many years. Nobody in the family has known.'

Shane, I like to think, still managed a bite of sandwich at this point. Ann, I know, put her hand authoritatively upon the brown envelope bulging with correspondence. Somehow his mind had to be focused away from 'Doesn't ham and cheese and salad cream make a handsome combination?'

'Shane,' she continued, 'do you know what it is "to be adopted"?'

At this precise moment the minds of mother and youngest son began to follow very different courses. For Ann this was the moment when, for the second time, she was about to tell one of her beloved children the most sacred truth of her entire life. Shane, however, eyes wide open, believed he was about to be given the answer to the most sacred riddle of his own life – 'Why am I six feet, four inches tall but my parents hardly reach my ribcage?'

'Jesus, Mam. What are you telling me?'

'That your daddy and I had a son adopted.'

'You had me adopted.'

'What? Not you, Shane. In this envelope I have a picture of your oldest brother.'

'You have a picture of Liam?'

'No.'

'Liam's not my big brother! Then I was adopted. Jeez, Mam, are we all adopted?'

'No, Shane. Paul. This is Paul.'

'Who's he then?'

Half an hour later Shane too had been led dutifully to the phone by Ann. He made a much better fist of a call to someone he'd never heard of thirty minutes ago – who was both eleven years older than him and his big brother – than I could have managed at his age. Once again in my journey there was an unexpected lingua franca established within moments, as we moved on to the subject of linear versus non-linear editing in the post-production of television programmes. But Shane was also the first of perhaps a hundred people to say, 'Fair play to you,' which was another example of two countries divided by a common language. I think I understand what it's meant to convey now, although I haven't ever truly found the context in which I might use it myself, even in Ireland. But coming from Shane it was graceful, generous, and promised a welcome in person yet to come.

Two days later it was the turn of the man who I still see as the oldest brother of the Brennan family, Liam. He is like Michael, an instinct player and, beneath a manly exterior, a gentle and nurturing man. He is also an electrician, was then a regular soccer player and (I'm pretty sure he would accept this as a fair description) an accomplished social drinker. He was also the father of two boys of similar ages to my own, although his oldest, Finian, was a year older than Jake. I was no electrician, and have never had a head for a piss-up more than once or twice a decade, but we were both fathers and we both loved soccer. Liam's opening line on the phone was a no-bullshit 'Fair play to you', and I probably made a bit of a monkey of myself reassuring him that I had no intention to swoop in as a replacement oldest brother to the Brennans. His general demeanour was so superbly laid back, yet simultaneously so astute, that if the thought had occurred to him he had clearly reckoned it was not a problem and not to be dwelled upon. I also felt myself much less accidentally threatening to any older brother status as Finian was already established as and remained the oldest grandchild.

In a sense Liam is the kind of man I would love to be for a trial week: a man of few words and all actions. I have a poor record with this personality type, having once gone out with a woman who was practically monosyllabic, and – unlike Liam – missing the part of the cortex containing the sense of humour. She had many other qualities, and I became intrigued by this Spartan use of language, this habit of watching my face in a film to know when to laugh. I became convinced that she was a latter-day Sphinx, that if I stuck with it I would discover an incredible, essential personality. I'm afraid I never did, which could well have been my own fault, but I did spend many evenings filling her sitting room with my hot air and withering from her almost complete lack of response. Since then I have had a terror of men or women of few words.

Although Liam and I got on well on the phone, it was with him more than the other children that I found my life in most pointed contrast. Liam would have been conceived not that long after I was born, so we really did run simultaneously along parallel tracks. At the age of eleven I was ecstatic to see the underdogs, Sunderland, beat Leeds United in the FA Cup Final; back in Dublin a nine-and-a-half-year-old, my brother, was crushed that his beloved Leeds could fail. I remember that day very well, because it was the first time I had flu, and I'd watched it in my pyjamas by the fire. I might have been in Dublin that day, sharing my brother's disappointment, and vowing, as he has done to this day, to support Leeds come what may. We talked about that on the phone.

None of my other new siblings had married and had children, but Liam was, like me, already a family man. On the phone he had the most pronounced Dublin accent of them all, which perhaps I would have had too, and when we rang off I felt the second pang of regret, after not having run last for Ireland. Liam would have been my playmate, perhaps my closest friend, but now he, like myself, was the father to two sons, who were each other's playmates and closest friends. Perhaps the earth had spun too many times for he and I ever to catch up.

I was also aware of a number of studies on the role of birth order in one's fate in future life. It was claimed that second children have, throughout history, been the revolutionaries in both ideas and action. Their older siblings naturally adhere more to the storyline as defined by the parents, and the little chap has to get himself noticed by making his own noise. This kind of speculation is beyond proof, yet all my life I had behaved like everyone's big brother. I was paternalistic even when I was eight or nine, and later in life I often felt like a king without a country, with a whole raft of innate abilities to build compromise and lead gentle action left rusting in a cupboard. So what of Liam – had he enjoyed the big brother role, or had he felt like a Gerald Ford, thrust unexpectedly into the spotlight? I'm sure he thinks it wouldn't have mattered, and it goes to show that with all adoption quests it is only possible to make sane progress if you refrain from playing what-might-have-beens.

Ann, meanwhile, was yet to learn that her buff envelope was not a prop to be casually deployed but had the explosive potential of a stick of dynamite. She had decided that Liam's wife, Anita, her only daughter-in-law, was owed a personal explanation as well. Once again she was at the kitchen table, once again she brandished the envelope, but this time, in order to illustrate her point, she withdrew a blazing colour photograph of me, and set it on the table in front of Anita.

'Anita, I have something very important to tell you. Do you see that photograph?'

Anita could of course see the photograph that, having been taken five years before, looked to her precisely like Liam in a very smart tailored suit and rich silk tie.

'Jesus, Ann, what are you showing me?' The colour had, apparently, drained from Anita's face.

'Well, Anita, it's a terrible secret but Michael and I don't want to keep it hidden any more. You see the young man in the photograph?'

'I do, Ann. I should know him – aren't I married to him myself? What's he doing in all that get-up. When was this picture taken? I just don't understand, Ann.'

'No, no, Anita, that's not Liam. That's Paul.'

'Don't tell me that, Ann, who's Paul? That's Liam all right. And when the hell did he have the time to marry her? Who's she, anyway?'

Standing boldly by my side, in one of the wedding day photographs I had brought to Dublin with me that weekend, was Lydia, radiant in an ivory bridal gown. The misunderstanding was now clear to Ann who, in accidentally leading her daughter-in-law to believe that her husband was a bigamist, had broken the ground so completely that the mere fact of having had a child put up for adoption was child's play by comparison.

That, therefore, was Liam, Maeve and Shane all done. Even if it was only on the telephone, our mother, my natural mother, Ann, had taken all our hands and clenched them together. She had begun to remake the bond. My final sibling, Barry, I did not speak to on the phone at all. I met him in person just one week later.

The previous summer these two words which now so preoccupied me – Ireland and Adoption – had no place in my conscious thought. This summer I was struggling with the meaning of both words. My best friend was clearly alarmed by what he must have worried was a serious conflict of identity. We went out one night and he spoke openly. He had known my parents for more than twenty years and he was fearful of their response when I eventually told them what had happened to me. He accepted, I believe, my moral and legal right to have acted as I had done thus far, but he knew my parents too well to believe that explaining this to them would go without opposition and hurt.

Cris was a good person to speak to about this. He had a residual affection for my parents, who had watched him over the years run about in our garden, puff Gauloises and choose as his holiday job the position of refuse collector for Bromley Council, which led him, in a moment that delighted his sense of social mischief, to be our bin man for a few weeks. He had also come to a number of soccer matches as my dad's guest, particularly on the rare occasions when his team, Chelsea, met ours, Charlton Athletic, and therefore had seen my dad at his best, doing what he enjoyed most, singing our club song 'When the Red Red Robin comes bob-bob-bobbin' along'.

But even Cris, with his head for jurisprudence, couldn't really help. His own parents were much more of the time than mine, and his house was always the one with the parties and the licensed smoking and the Bob Dylan records. He had never seen that when he returned to his house as a youth, having played snooker at mine, that he was heading back into the 1970s while my house was more like the 1950s. This is not intended as a criticism of my parents at all. Like most adoptive parents back then, they were in their late thirties and early forties when they had me, and they had suffered things in the Second World War that my pampered generation could only read about. My father had been with the British Army crossing the Rhine and had been into the concentration camps, and my mother had huddled in south London bomb shelters while the Luftwaffe poured death across the city in hundreds of tons of explosives. They had both seen some terrible things, and had been part of a generation who only survived the decade after the war through rationing, self-sacrifice and a rigid adherence to the social mores of the day, which mostly had their origin still from late Victorian or early Edwardian values.

Neither Cris nor I were destined to have the experience that my parents had had of infertility and the inability to conceive. Cris and I have been blessed with eight children between us to date, and have never experienced that heart-rending moment when a doctor shakes his head and asks if you have ever considered adoption. The period of disappointment, followed by waiting, followed by the miracle of a child becoming available and then being approved for adoption, is of a completely different order to an easy conception, nine months of anticipation and the ultimate joy of the birth of your own child. And finally I was aware that both of my parents had adored, revered, idolised their own mothers and fathers. I was grateful to my parents, and I loved them in my own way, but my feelings were never as potent or reverential as that. Looking at it now, I sometimes wonder how my feelings could reasonably have been expected to be otherwise. I said to Cris that I would tell them, but not yet.

After an hour of heavy discussion Cris asked the question that really seemed to be preying on his mind: 'Let's say there's a World Cup qualifier between Ireland and England,' he began, 'which team are you going to support?'

I wasn't offended by his question, but I was astonished that he felt it necessary to ask. 'England,' I replied. 'For God's sake, Cris, who did you think I'd support?'

He seemed very relieved. I'm pretty sure that it was not the question of national affiliation that concerned him, but the idea that his best friend might wake up one morning as, what is known, so Liam tells me, a Plastic Paddy. Yet every time I heard the word adoption it seemed to involve some issue of nationality or ethnicity, gender or some other mark of identity. There were 700,000 female children awaiting adoption in China. It wasn't that the Chinese didn't value the female sex, but that a female child would be less able to look after you when you grew old, and if you were only allowed one live birth per couple you had to ensure it was a boy. The result was hundreds of thousands of abandoned girls every year. This problem has not disappeared today.

A few weeks or so before I would have turned the page on this story and been left untouched. Now I felt helpless in the scale of this present-day tragedy. I had learned that there were probably about 700,000 adopted children from my own pre-1975, pre-open-adoption period alive in England and Wales, stretching right back to Edwardian times. In China, the same number were looking for mums and dads right now, even as I sipped my cup of tea. Their massive problem had also been mine – social orthodoxy and sexual intercourse are not good partners, for while you might remember the sexual intercourse for the rest of your life, it only lasted minutes. Not so the decades and centuries of political or religious dogma.

In the United Kingdom it was widely debated whether it was best always to have a child of African ethnicity adopted only into a black family. As a means of educating the child to protect itself against racial abuse and prejudice, this seemed sound enough, but too many representatives for this argument seemed to have wider agendas, describing the white man as an oppressor and the black child handed to the white, affluent middle classes as no more than a latter-day market purchase, a new slave. In the children's homes and in short-term fostering, meanwhile, a generation of young black and mixed race children were forgotten, and in the suburbs those whose hearts had already been broken by their infertility were denied an opportunity to be their loving parents.

In America the One Church, One Child programme set up in Chicago by the Reverend George H. Clements sought to recruit black adoptive parents through local churches. In America the black experience with many bureaucracies had been unsatisfactory, and dealings with the adoption system had left many potential adoptive parents excluded. The mission of One Church, One Child was to combine the resources of the church and the state to provide black adoptive parents for black adopted children. The motivation was compassionate, not political – to serve the needs of the three points of the black Adoption Triangle. In the coming years, with the burgeoning of evangelical church missions among the Afro-Caribbean communities in the UK, a movement such as this could do much good work. That summer, though, and sadly still today, this issue was played out in local authority social services departments. When they were good they were very, very good, but when they were bad . . .

In relation to what I now had to accept was my own ethnicity, but not by any means my identity, I found the news of the Irish in London a matter of some concern. A survey had shown a spectacularly high rate of suicide among young Irish men in London, and among the older men an astonishingly high rate of heart disease and liver damage, caused not from some ethnic malfunction but by habits of smoking and drinking that seemed to have been entirely untouched by any public health campaign.

The weekend after my first trip to Dublin I took Jake, yet again, to the casualty department of Lewisham Hospital, to have another gash patched up. He was fine, but coming out of the hospital on a sunny, Sunday after-noon on to the broad, tree-lined road outside we encoun-tered a titanically drunken man. Usually I would not have noticed his nationality, but his Irish accent was foaming out of his mouth.

'That's a lovely kid you have there, mister.' I thanked him. 'I miss my own daddy myself, sir. You take care of him now.'

I said that I would and side-stepped him with Jake, who asked me what was wrong with the man who was now stag-gering across the busy road. I said that he was sad and missed his home country. Jake, of course, asked me which country, and I told him – Ireland.

'You went to Ireland, Daddy.'

'I did, darling, but the men are mostly happy there.' I had given him his feed line.

'Why don't they stay there then?'

I thought about my answer, and told him that when that man was young there would have been little work for him in Ireland and he had to come to England. But he might have left his family behind, and found friends only in pubs, where he developed a mighty capacity for drink. In these pubs they played only Irish music, and this reminded him of his sorrow at no longer being in his home country, which made him drink even more. Jake thought about this.

'Does Ata go to Iranian pubs and get drunk?'

Ata is a friend of ours who has been in the UK for twenty years, having left Iran. He is married to another good friend, with three children. He had just got his Ph.D.

'No,' I replied, 'Ata doesn't do that.'

'Then why do the Irish do it?'

That was enough explanation for one day. In any case, I didn't know the answer. And I wasn't about to make excuses for an ethnic group I had only just joined.

A week later I was on my way back up to Stansted Airport, this time in the car. Ann was still on a fantastic roll and had decided that it was time to come over to London. She had two reasons. Barry, my third sibling, had graduated in law from Trinity, Dublin that summer, and I now learned he was in London doing various jobs while he attempted to get a position as part of the in-house legal team of a London bank, at which he soon succeeded. Ann was extremely close to Barry, and it seemed that he had always been her assiduous, loyal and undiluted supporter. She felt she could not possibly just ring him in his Neasden flat and drop the news of my existence into his ear down a telephone line. She wanted to do so in person.

Her second reason for coming was that she had a daughter-in-law and two grandsons to meet. I took Jake with me to the airport. In part, of course, I loved spending time with him whenever, and he was good company on the journey, but in another part he would also give me a bit of a cushion. From speaking to Ann on the phone, her emotions were running in great loops above the Palmerstown sky. I was incredibly glad to see her, and becoming very fond of her, but I still couldn't react on that epic scale myself. I probably hoped that the deployment of a grandchild might take the heat out from under me a little bit.

I'd had another long conversation with Maeve, and she'd told me that since my weekend in Dublin Ann had seemed twenty years younger. Maeve said that there were many moments in her own childhood when she would steal a look at Ann and see some unfathomable regret, and that all of this now seemed to have been spirited away. She was right. Ann had spent hours praying for me, remembering my birthday in silence, lighting candles, and even wondering whether Irish-looking English newsreaders on UK television picked up in Dublin were in fact me. Coming through arrivals at Stansted, she was practically exploding with smiles. (She was also smoking, her only concession to addiction. That weekend Lydia, Ann and I must have smoked two hundred cigarettes, and I don't smoke.)

In the days that followed Ann and I realised that we had been extraordinarily lucky because of our shared associations with Blackheath. On the morning after her arrival we set out on a walk from my house, crossing the Lee High Road, up Glenton Road where I lived when I met

Lydia, and through Heath Lane to emerge on to Blackheath itself. Every foot of this walk is saturated with associations for me, and every foot of this walk was also redolent for my new mother. Perhaps, in this millennial era, there has been enough said about the significance of Greenwich Park and the history of time, but I will never stop loving it, and to walk through its gates and along its meridian line, accompanied by a woman with whom I had just re-emerged from my own time capsule, seemed quite perfect. There is no place else I would rather have walked with her that day.

Greenwich Park itself always has an unusually high representation of people from beyond the shores of England. Tourists from all over the world come down the Thames from Westminster for a day trip on a riverboat, but the travellers I believe affect the atmosphere of the park most are the many parties of teenagers from northern Europe whose coaches stop outside the park gates. Usually they are either on their way back from a school trip to London, or making their first stopping point after crossing the English Channel. Whichever group they belong to, one can always sense that they are absorbing the magic of the park.

For the groups on the way home, it is green space and escarpment at last, after hours of foot-numbing trips around the National Gallery. It is a change, an opportunity to be among real Londoners – not office workers and tour guides, but lovers, soccer players and parents with children. For the groups arriving in London, they can see their destination set out before them from the hill by the statue of General Wolfe. On every walk through the park one can see these teenagers linking arms, holding hands, kissing and, most of all, laying down memories of a place they will never forget.

On this walk, Ann and I were laying down new memories of a place we had both known well. Ann could realistically have expected never to see Blackheath or Greenwich again, and I could have expected only to have thousands more walks in the park there with our children, with the occasional faint, miserable resonance of my life before I met Lydia. There was no issue of national identity at all. Indeed, it seemed absurd among all these foreign tongues. It was a mother and a son who had lost each other and been reunited before it was too late.

When we left the park and walked south towards Blackheath Village Ann was confronted by her past sins in the most bold way possible – literally in red neon lighting. It would be indelicate to re-imagine the night of my conception (let's keep some taboos here), but I do know that it ran its course in the Clarendon Hotel, Blackheath, the large sign for which one can see across the entire grass-covered plateau. I have missed hundreds of open goals within spitting distance of the Clarendon Hotel, and while I would not wish to malign its fine facilities for social and conference events today, one can imagine that its register still sees an overnight stay from the occasional Mr and Mrs Smith.

The effect for me that day, this day, and every day until I move from this area, is that where once I did not know who my natural parents were or from whence they came, now I drive past the red neon sign marking the precise point of my conception every day of my life.

We carried on down into Tranquil Vale and up the hill on the other side. Here we emerged into an area that had even more fixed roots to Ann's past than I had realised. The first turning on the left after the Blackheath Concert Halls is Blackheath Park, a road marking the beginning of the extensive private roads of the Cator Estate. All I had known about Ann's nursing career was that she had trained, but seeing where we were now she soon realised that we were about to pass The Gables, the turn-of-the-century nursing home where she was working when she conceived me. This must have been astonishing for her – I don't think she expected to trip across this place so easily – and the memories flooded back. Of back pain from moving elderly ladies in and out of bed, of the kitchen and its food and its friendly atmosphere, and of an English friend she'd had there, in whom she confided about her unexpected pregnancy, a friend who counselled her that she should undergo an abortion.

And memories came back to her too of Michael and her at a time when they were both mad for dancing and living life as fast as they could away from the grey skies of Eamonn de Valera's puritanical, post-war Ireland. Again, it is not my role to be indiscreet, but from the Michael that Ann described that day, he had never been a young man, in all respects, who took no for an answer.

We came back out into Lee Road, and walked straight ahead into Lee Terrace, which becomes Belmont Hill and runs the mile or so down into the centre of Lewisham. About seventy yards later we were standing by 48 Lee Terrace, or we would have been if it had not been demolished and replaced with a row of modern terraced houses typical of Blackheath in the sixties and seventies. The new houses are set back from the road behind a brick wall, and where the front of the building of number 48 would have been there is now a small patch of grass. Ann and I sat down, looked at each other, and laughed. She glanced towards the pavement and stood up.

'You know, I think it was right here that I went into labour. I can certainly remember the ambulance pulling up here.' She pointed to a spot at the side of the road. 'I can't remember it all for you. I'm sorry. I just recall that it was a very long journey to the other side of the river, to a nursing home.'

I mentioned the address of the home where I now knew I had been born – 262 Victoria Park Road, Hackney.

'That was it. You must think me dreadful, what with you being with Lydia at the boys' births and speaking so well about it, but I've just blanked the rest out. I was so scared.'

She seemed then to retrieve a lost memory, which told of a fact that I'd already guessed from what I had read of cases like hers.

'I remember . . . I remember the baby was born, sorry Paul, you were born. And they just took you away. I didn't even catch so much as a look at you. They took you out of the room and I never saw you again.'

The hardest of hearts would have begun to cry.

And so we walked on, down Brandram Road, along Glenton Road again, and the flat where Lydia refused to sleep more than once (some grumble about grey sheets), until we reached home, where Lydia had made a splendid salad and laid the table in the back garden for lunch. As we came in through the front door Jake had that look about him, the one that has connected two streams of thought and formulated a big question. Ann sat at the table outside, and Jake followed her and sat by her while Lydia and I fetched drink from the kitchen. Moments later we heard Ann laugh.

'Paul, you'll never believe what Jake just said. He said that I'm to eat as much as I like because we have nothing to eat in Ireland. What have you been telling him?'

'Ah, well I did mention the Potato Famine.'

'But that was a hundred and fifty years ago. He said that we gave you away because we were like the starving in Africa and had no food to give you to eat!'

I realised that I should have taken the time to complete my earlier brief history of Ireland for Jake, and not stopped until I'd hit the boom time of the Celtic Tiger. I also realised, once again, that while for me, at the still epicentre, my adoption story made perfect sense, it was a matter that could be misinterpreted very easily if I did not make it completely plain, wasn't completely open about it, myself. If I didn't tell the whole story other people would soon join the dots and make from them some entirely unrecognisable beast.

While this walk, bathed in July sunshine and the sweet scents of a past where now we both could go, was set in a location so apt that I could not have thought of anywhere better, the setting for my first ever meeting with one of my siblings was so unsuitable that it seems, even now, quite surreal.

After lunch Ann decided that she should phone Barry at his flat in Neasden and tell him she was over in London on a surprise visit. Although this already palpably rang untrue for Barry, he was pleased that his mum was nearby and agreed to meet later that evening. Ann told him at first that she was staying with some cousins in Romford, so Barry went to characteristic trouble in checking the route from Romford to Neasden, one that even a London cabby might scratch his head over. I watched this procedure in quiet amazement as Ann turned the page to take more completely unnecessary directions, and was not surprised when Barry ultimately doubted that he could direct her all the way to his front door. Finally it was agreed that she would be driven by one of these Irish cousins and ring from their mobile phone on approaching Barry's area.

Two hours later I was driving Ann (and Jake) up the Kilburn High Road, dialling Barry's number on my mobile, which I hurriedly passed to Ann. (I've got a feeling I was meant to be Barry's Uncle Sean, or perhaps his cousin Young Dennis; I've never been quite sure on this detail.) Barry answered and was reassured that his mother would soon be travelling north up Cricklewood Broadway. The nirvana of Neasden would not be far beyond. Ann suddenly looked at me and said (as if talking to an Irish relative), 'Do you know Staples Corner?' I nodded, mutely, although in an emergency I could have done a good impression based on Mr O'Brian the dentist.

Ann continued, 'We're to find a place called Chiquita's, and Barry will meet me in there in thirty minutes.' I nodded again. She gave the phone back to me and I flipped it shut.

Perhaps once, many years ago, there was a lovely old market gardener called Percy Staples, but he wouldn't find much top soil left at Staples Corner today. It is an especially busy and massive road junction where the North Circular Road, the Edgware Road out of London and the M1 meet. It is across the way from London's first shopping megalopolis, Brent Cross. It was probably mostly built by sons of Ireland, but it is a place devoid of any redeeming visual features. It also stinks of traffic fumes.

We made it to Staples Corner in ten minutes, so we had to kill time in a McDonald's car park for another twenty minutes before Ann calculated she should go into Chiquita's and wait for Barry. I imagined the plan was for

me to sit in the car with Jake, await her return, and meet
Barry at some future family reunion in Ireland. She had
only been gone for five minutes, however, when she came
toddling back out again.

'Isn't he there yet? Do you want to ring him again on
the phone?' I offered.

'No, he was in there. He's never late, Barry. So will you
come in then and we can all get something to eat?'

'What? Who am I meant to be?'

'You're Paul Arnott.'

'Ah, right, phew.'

'And you're his brother. I've told him everything. You're
not to worry. He's taken it very well and he really wants to
meet you.'

'You've told him I'm out here in the car?'

'Yes. Come on then.'

Chiquita's – speciality: taco shells, chilli con carne and
fajitas – was a plastic Mexico. As I entered with Ann and
Jake I felt quite absurd, like Clint Eastwood's man with no
name. ('Ma mammee says you're my brother. But you ain't
no kin of mine. Eat dust, varmint.') The illusion was height-
ened by the utter, desolate emptiness of the place. It was so
early it wasn't even happy hour yet. Barry was nowhere to
be seen. My left eyebrow raised a centimetre.

'He'll have just gone to the toilet,' said Ann calmly.

'Are you sure he's not legging it out of the window?'

'Calm down,' she replied, lighting a cigarette. 'Barry has
a good head on his shoulders.'

We took the table where the ghost of Barry's discussion
with his mother – two teacups and a stubbed-out cigarette
– lay undisturbed. The three of us sat down in the near
darkness of the banquetted table, and I looked at the menu
to see which chilli-laced dish I might persuade Jake to eat
for his supper. I offered him a menu to study too, and he
decided he would take it with him under the table. He is a
glorious child, one of the lights of my life, but in a tense,
life-changing moment such as this I could depend upon
him to behave to my maximum discomfort. And so he did,
and as my brother Barry – flesh and blood, incarnate –
walked out of the loo towards us, Jake hit his head on the
underneath of the table and began to cry. So it was that I
met the first of my long-lost siblings with a four-year-old
wriggling in my arms, animating the heavy silence of
Chiquita's with a piercing scream. A hug with my new
sibling, even a handshake, was not possible.

Barry's handling of this extraordinary moment was as
faultless as Maeve's and Shane's had been on the phone.
The special degree of difficulty facing him, however – with
this bizarre *High Noon* setting, a hungry, grumpy four-
year-old and the five minutes to absorb the fact that his
mother had given birth to a child before Liam – earned
him much extra credit in my eyes. He didn't just cope, he
welcomed me, said that whatever his mother and father
wanted was what he wanted too. Yet again I made my super-
fluous speech about not wanting to threaten the order of
the family, not intending in any way to be territorial. He

listened patiently, but I realised that the reason he and the other children had no fear that I would disrupt their family was that they each knew, with complete conviction, that the family structure was so well constructed, so tested, that it was beyond disruption from outside. I could have turned up as a rotter with the express intention of blackmailing their parents and they would have held together regardless.

I have no idea what Barry made of me on first meeting, but within nanoseconds my brain had instinctively computed the parts of his face and body that he had drawn from either Ann or Michael, and what parts of him were variations of the me I knew in the mirror. I had Michael's short nose, Barry had Ann's pointed, stronger nose. He had Ann's underlying facial bone structure, I had none (Michael's). His hair was exactly the colour mine had been nine years before, his arms and chest as hairy. He was maybe an inch shorter, slim and swift. His blue eyes were like a precise blend of Ann and Michael's, mine were very much Ann's. I had an English Received Pronunciation accent from the bass end of the range, and he – well, to be very honest, when I first met him I thought he sounded like the jockey Willie Carson. Later he joked that people sometimes thought he was a woman when he answered the phone. I dare mention this now only because Barry has since spent half a decade in London and, while rightly retaining his accent, has moved his voice many notches nearer to Lee Marvin's. That day in Chiquita's, the difference in our voices struck a chord.

But what I most noticed, what most endured about Barry, was that he was perceptive and empathetic. I would have welcomed inbreds from a muddy farmyard but having siblings with fine minds was another unsought bonus. I had now met the first of the reflections in the four-panelled mirror. It was one of which I could not have been more proud.

The next day, Sunday, Barry came over to lunch in Lewisham. There is in such a situation another benefit in having been raised Irish. I still believe that I will never fully be able to communicate to them the nervousness of an Englishman when he enters another man's castle, especially if he feels the ground beneath his feet has the potential to shift. Barry, whose childhood house had entertained hundreds of friends, politicians and half-known members of family up from the country, had no inhibitions in a strange social setting, even when he joined me on the meet-a-complete-stranger rollercoaster when Ann introduced him to Lydia, Jake and Benjamin.

It was with Barry that day that I began to appreciate, with gratitude to the fates, that my timing in coming into this family's life, quite by accident, had been perfect. I was thirty-two, Barry was twenty-three and a graduate. He was a grown-up. If I had appeared when I was twenty-seven Barry would have been eighteen – I a grown-up, he barely more than a child, albeit one who in photographs seemed to have had shoulder-length hair tied back in a ponytail, à la *Commitments*. But this confident, funny and wise Trinity law graduate eating my roast chicken was ready for the big, bad world, and more than ready for me. Over lunch I began to entertain the oddest fantasies – perhaps the Brennans were a latter-day Kennedy family who had mislaid their JFK? Barry was perfect casting for Robert Kennedy – legally and socially minded, raised in a political family. Perhaps all I had to do was persuade Lydia to uproot to Ireland, where I could claim the keys to Camelot. On the other hand, perhaps my long years in England had rendered me more Edward than Jack. The grass is greener in Ireland, but even in this early meeting with two members of my full-blood family, I knew, and was saddened, that London's loveless grasp would never release me.

Whenever I pass into trans-fatty acid territory at McDonald's (and within weeks I would again, just before meeting the next sibling) I would die rather than order a Mc – anything, especially if it's a dish like the McRib. Even if the assistant challenges me with, 'You want a McRib?' I hold my ground, an example to my children. 'Yes. A rib. Thank you.' So it was that Barry and I discovered a difference in our use of language that I immediately knew, even if I were standing for the Irish presidency, I could never yield to. I asked Barry if he'd like a drink, meaning a cold drink.

'Ah no, a mineral would be fine.'

'Still or sparkling?'

'What flavours do you have?'

'Er – water flavour. But you can have it gassy or without.'

'Do you not have any orange?'

'Fresh orange juice, of course.'

'No, like, do you have an orange mineral?'

'Er – I'm not sure. Why don't you have a look in the fridge?'

'You keep it in the refrigerator? Should I just look in this cupboard?' He took a look inside and emerged satisfied with a bottle of saccharine-filled orange and mango concentrate we had left over from a kid's tea party.

'Oh, right,' I said, placing two types of water and Tropicana orange juice back in the fridge. 'You actually want that stuff, not "a mineral".'

Barry looked at me as if I were a man from Atlantis. 'This is a mineral.'

'You call that a mineral? I see.'

'What do you call it?'

'Orange squash. But, I mean, you couldn't really go calling it a mineral in London. Chemically it's many things, but mineral is not one of them.'

I know this sounds a touch pompous, but what else could I bequeath a new brother if not a few insights into the local vernacular. And then I remembered, all those Olde Tea Shoppes I had been taken to as a young child, and there on the menu, opposite Welsh Rarebit and Toasted Teacake, were 'Minerals' – Orange, Lemon and, in top tea shops, Rose's Lime Cordial. I don't remember using the term myself, even then, thinking that minerals were found in rock formations, but here was Barry, whose big concern at college had been European environmental law, using the word mineral for this flavoured syrup. Ireland was a country I knew even less than I had thought. I might catch up with my family, but could I ever catch up with this place across the sea?

8

Dancing the New

THE REUNION with my natural parents in that first weekend in Dublin could reasonably be described as a low-level security operation. As such it failed almost before it started when I became the focus of the unhappy gaze of hundreds of striking marchers. But the rest of that weekend had gone without a hitch, though I'd known Michael had a few explanations up his sleeve if we'd bumped into someone at the theatre or in the church. I was to have been 'a friend from London'.

I am all the fonder of Barry for his often expressed view since then that his parents should have acted as if they were prepared to take out a full-page advert in the *Irish Independent*, announcing that they had now acquired an interest in a fifth child. The logic of this view is irrefutable, but the actual process of detoxifying a century of secrets and lies is mired in complexities. That my emergence into the acknowledged life of the Brennans was cautiously done actually made it easier for me. I felt unrushed. In addition, the security operation in Dublin had unwittingly acclimatised me to the byzantine activity surrounding my first ever meeting with Maeve.

Three weeks had passed since I had first met Ann and Michael, and I had not dreamed that I could possibly expect to meet Maeve so soon. There was in this another, geographical, contrast in cultures – English against Irish. Even today I still think of passenger flight as either a luxury item or a business trip. I collect my reward points at Sainsbury's with Scrooge-like ruthlessness, anally converting them to Air Miles at the earliest possible moment, engorged with pleasure when my statement comes through, oozing six or seven thousand unused Air Miles. And even though I have acquired these riches simply by doing the normal family shopping at Sainsbury's, Lee Green, where I have been going anyway for over fifteen years (shopping for six, including nappies, earns reward points beyond the dreams of avarice) I will not spend them. What if we have to fly somewhere in an emergency, I caution Lydia. She has ignored me and flown portions of the family to Frankfurt, Bordeaux and Toulouse in recent years, while I have gathered dust at home. Doesn't she realise we could have had fifteen thousand Air Miles in the bank? All she can do is waste them on taking flights.

But my own paralysis has not afflicted the young, modern Irish, who seem to take as many flights as they do car journeys. Maeve had been criss-crossing over my head since her schooldays and a weekend trip to London was absolutely nothing to her. Her boyfriend, Lar, had a sister who was working at the Cumberland Hotel by Marble Arch, and the pair were coming to visit her, affording an opportunity for Maeve and me to meet for the first time.

Not so simple, though. Although Maeve had already told Lar of my existence she was still under orders from Ann and Michael *not* to have told him. More crucially, there was no way I could meet Lar if this meeting was to predate a meeting with either Liam or Shane for the first time. And Lar obviously couldn't tell his sister that Maeve was about to meet her brother from England, because that would be departing even further from the current strategy from Palmerstown.

In these circumstances, and with the benefit of hindsight, the lobby of the Cumberland Hotel was not the most discreet place to meet. There was a complex cluster of reasons why, connected with Maeve's knowledge of that part of London, her luggage being in the hotel, and her departure to meet her cousins in Romford later that afternoon. I left Lydia and the children at home having lunch (we were to meet at 1.30 p.m.) and caught the train and the tube up to Marble Arch. I arrived at 1.05 p.m. London is an almost impossible city in which to kill time without spending money, which is why gentlemen and ladies invented clubs for themselves, but I did my best on this sunny afternoon.

I looked around me at Marble Arch, past the stalls selling policeman's helmets and toy double-decker buses, and wandered across the road to Speakers' Corner. Sunday morning is the time to be here these days, but at Saturday lunchtime I didn't even recognise the language being spoken, other than to identify it as Middle Eastern and involving stamping on the Stars and Stripes. I was in a short-lived phase when I was deluding myself that I was the living solution to Anglo-Irish discord, being from both the houses of Montague and Capulet. I was well aware, though, that even I would never have anything to offer to build bridges between the invisible forces of the Pentagon and the inflamed opponents of US foreign policy around the world.

I looked away from the speaker and north again, through the trees towards the massive Odeon cinema at Marble Arch. The Odeon, for a long time the most technically advanced cinema in London, was the place where I would see the James Bond movies of my teenage years, from the unconfined joy of *Live and Let Die* to the flaccid flop of *Moonraker*. Even in my artistic twenties, when I could have had a season ticket to the Lumiere Cinema and its subtitled treats, I still snuck off to Marble Arch to see *Licence to Kill* with Lydia. But today the Odeon Marble Arch meant a thousand times more to me than ever before. For Michael had told me a story of his early days in London before he met Ann, when weather and pollution occasionally combined to create a dense smog across the city. He was due to have been fitting some huge engine in a factory east of London but a smog had descended and all public transport was cancelled, so he could not get to work. By midday the smog was clearing, but the machine work for the day had been postponed. Michael was left with an afternoon to himself in London.

Like just about every young man of his age, Irish or English, he had an unfulfilled love for any film about the Wild West, cowboys, the big country. So Michael entered the Odeon Marble Arch, leaving the soot and fumes behind him on the street, and bought a matinee ticket for one of the first British screenings of *Oklahoma*. He told me this story with his eyes burning bright – that the film had already started, that the screen was set up for full colour cinemascope, which he had not seen before, and that as he walked through the door into the cinema itself he walked into that glorious opening scene where the happiest cowboy ever born sings 'Oh What A Beautiful Morning'. Michael told me he really felt that he could have walked up that cinema aisle and into the middle of the bright golden haze on the meadow. I loved this story, its contrast with the London outside, the capacity for fantasy of the young man who fathered me. And I loved it because, in hushed and gentle tones, I had been singing 'Oh What A Beautiful Morning' to Jake and Benjamin since they had both been born.

Still, I couldn't stand gawping at the Odeon, Marble Arch, so I retreated to McDonald's on Oxford Street where, almost immediately, I had one of those Winnie-The-Pooh moments. On the one hand, it was 1.15 p.m., lunchtime, and in a whole quarter of an hour there was plenty of time to eat a cheeseburger and a cup of tea. On the other hand I was about to meet the sister I had never met and, having felt self-conscious about my extra weight and lost a few pounds, I wanted to look my Slim Jim best. But you know how it is – I was sort of swept towards the counter, and anyway, isn't there a by-law against nursing just a cup of tea at lunchtime?

At 1.30 p.m. precisely I entered the Cumberland wiping cheeseburger, chocolate milkshake and apple pie from the corners of my mouth. For some reason I felt a bit lardy. As per my secret instructions I went to the phone in the lobby, rang room number four hundred and something, and waited for it to answer. The lobby seemed simultaneously to be welcoming and checking out two coachloads of tourists and had the fevered atmosphere of a souk. Maeve answered; if she was half as nervous as me then her knees must have been knocking like Michael Flatley's, but she seemed calm.

'All right, Paul. Are you there? I'll come straight down but we'll have to leave the lobby straightaway. Yes, Romford, is it on the Central line?'

This dialogue didn't seem to make entire sense from where I was standing. I hazarded a guess. 'Maeve, is there someone else in the room with you?'

'Hahaha,' she answered, before whispering, 'I have Lar's

sister practically standing on top of me. She wants to go for a coffee. Oh Jimmy Mac.' She went back up to normal volume, 'Lar, why don't the two of you go off together? Don't be worrying about me, I need to go to Boots.' Sotto voce once more, 'Jeez, Paul, how will I know you?'

'Have you seen the photographs?'

'Ah, that'd be all right.'

'Just add a stone. Look, I'll know you. Don't worry.'

In Dublin, a stranger in a strange land, this sort of Secret Squirrel behaviour had a perverse logic, but it was bizarre to find myself still behaving this way in my home town. It's one thing keeping a low profile in Dublin, but ducking behind pillars in a London hotel made me feel like a low-rent, private dick following an errant wife. I rather enjoyed it.

Two minutes later there she was, coming out of the lift – my sister. The first-impressions processor was cranking furiously, just as it had with Barry. Thick brown/black hair, that more pointed nose again, and those facial bones. Smiling blue eyes, which for a minute blinked so nervously that I thought I had a sister with a twitch. A brilliant smile, one that I recognised must sometimes have endured periods of pain, like a very pretty Spike Milligan. And this time I got a hug.

It didn't matter what we did next just so long as we got out of the hotel lobby and the risk of being seen. I asked Maeve if she'd like to go somewhere for a cup of tea. Finding a quiet corner of a restaurant in Oxford Street would have been impossible, so I grabbed her arm and led her across the insane traffic of Marble Arch, back into the north-east corner of Hyde Park. As a student I'd worked at Harrods for nine different stretches, and on each of these hundreds and hundreds of days I had retreated to Hyde Park at lunchtime to read. Every now and then, if I was meeting a friend from school or a girlfriend, we'd take a boat out on the Serpentine and finish with tea at the water-side café.

That was where Maeve and I headed that day. I was so excited that I wanted to skip as we approached the terrace in front of the curved, seventies-designed, single-storey, glass and concrete building. Of all my siblings, Maeve was the one who I had found it most difficult to believe would actually exist beyond a photograph. As a man without a sister I'd considered that any woman made from the same matter as me must surely resemble a lady wrestler. It was incredible to be sitting down opposite this pretty young woman, the one sibling who'd lived her life not only on parallel tracks, but as a different sex.

Her first-impressions processor had worked instantly too. As we sat opposite each other she assessed me from top to toe in under a second.

'I'd say you're a Jones all right.'

'What does that mean?'

'It's in your eyes, they come from Mam's side. Like Uncle Noel has these very blue eyes. And you have a look of Liam about you too, though actually you're very different.'

I can't remember which of Maeve's questions I replied to with a lecture rather than a concise answer, but this made her think again.

'Hold on there. You look like Mam, but you sound like Dad. I'd say you're very like him.'

'So what does that mean?'

'Well, you know all about Dad's union work? And he'd be an MEP now if the votes had been counted first past the post rather than PR.'

'So how am I like him? I'm not politically active at all. Though I know I should be.'

'Now you see that's just the kind of thing Dad would say. He likes a laugh but he's never too far from what's serious, what he believes in. I'd say you're like that too.'

If Maeve and I had met as strangers on a train we could have spoken for a week, but as it was, with three decades or so to catch up on, the conversation really did flow like wine and ran even faster when Maeve revealed that she too had some news. She explained that after she'd had chemotherapy for her cancer of the stomach she'd been told that she might have difficulty ever conceiving a child. And then she'd got the all-clear, and she and Lar had felt in the mood for a celebration.

'Anyway, I've some news for you, big brother. Your sister's going to have a baby, what do you think of that?'

I grabbed her hand. 'That is absolutely brilliant.'

She laughed. 'Uncle Paul, eh? How does that sound to you? Which also means that I'm to invite you and Lydia to a wedding. Lar and I were to marry anyhow but this little event has brought it all forward. We're going for it the month after next.'

'God, we'd love to come. But won't there be a problem? I'm not saying I look exactly like Barry or anything, but . . . who will I be at the wedding?'

'You're to be yourself, my brother, and if anybody doesn't like it then fuck 'em.'

'So you're continuing the family tradition.'

'How do you mean?'

'Of walking up the aisle as three rather than two. We went in for that ourselves. As, we now know, did Ann and Michael.'

'Yes, and I'm not saying anything, but I think Liam and Anita had to get a move on at one stage too.'

'So what that means is that in the three decades since the Brennan/Jones coupling of 1961 the family will have created five oldest children and the dates don't add up on any of them.'

'Isn't the whole thing a bloody madness? I'm just really sorry that you got so badly caught up in it at a time when it was all such a stupid mess.'

'Yes. Look, you know I don't regret my life, don't you?'

'Jeez, I know that all right, Paul. You're a good man.'

'But just because I don't regret it, it doesn't stop this moment meeting you from being one of the most best moments of my life. It's something I could never have imagined.'

'Ah, give over. Would you share another bar of choco-late?'

Sadly Romford was calling too soon and it was time for us to walk back to the Cumberland Hotel. We strolled along with linked arms. For the first time I really felt like someone's older brother. There was this marvellous piece of work by my side, a fully grown pretty pride of Irish womanhood, and if I bumped into someone I knew I could say, boast, that I was her brother. As we said goodbye I urged her to say hello to Lar from me, to congratulate him, and thank him for inviting me to his wedding.

'All right then, bro. See you at the wedding?'

'Wouldn't miss it for anything.'

'It should be some craic all right.'

And blazing a characteristic trail my new sister vanished into the Oxford Street crowd.

One-third of our lives asleep, one-tenth eating, though in my case, since I've become father to four, those figures seem to have reversed. The figure I'd be fascinated to see in the audit of life is what fraction we spend doing silly things that we conceal from those closest to us. As a child there was the air guitar, the bedroom boxing match against Joe Bugner, the Churchillian maiden speech to parliament, the easy seduction of Raquel Welch, the saving of Katy Northwood as she lay tied to the railway lines at Beckenham Junction. Do we know that we've grown up when we leave this solitary fantasising behind us?

So why, when Lydia went to bed that Saturday night, did I slither to the video shelf? Why did I let her think I was watching cricket highlights when in fact I was pushing the play button on a video of the first ever transmission of *Riverdance*? This wasn't the show that became the most successful touring stadium event in the world, but the original seven-minute entertainment that was the home country's interval piece when the Eurovision Song Contest came to Ireland earlier in the year.

When Ann had come to London this tape had been one of her gifts, along with the jeroboam of Bailey's from duty-free. I'd heard the talk about this *Riverdance* thing in the ether, but it seemed to be the Daily Mail/Radio Two constituency who were most excited about it and I hadn't grasped it at all. On the first evening of Ann's visit she asked if I'd like to watch it and I agreed out of politeness and with some dread. The box cover said 'Riverdance for Rwanda' and as a package it seemed to be a typically Irish good deed, aimed at recycling a small proud moment for charity. On its cover was a two-shot of Jean Butler, looking pretty enough but unremarkable, and Michael Flatley in a Spanish waiter's outfit, sporting the last mullet haircut in the Western world. Its provenance as an entertainment born from the loins of the Eurovision Song Contest completed the prospect of utter naffness. I pressed play. Seven minutes later I turned to my new old mother and said, 'Bloody hell, that was absolutely fantastic.'

'Did you like it? I hoped you would. I love it altogether myself. Did I tell you we were there?'

'You were there?'

'Ah, Michael's always being invited to these things. It was held at The Point, have you heard of that? We were the guests of Michael D. Higgins, do you know about him?'

I did know about him. He had the title of Minister for Arts, Culture and the Gaeltacht, and at the time he was becoming famous for the raft of tax incentives that had lured movies like *Braveheart* to shoot in Ireland. (Michael D., as he was known, also lent Mel Gibson the Irish Army to play the bewigged band of hairy-arsed Scots rampaging through the heather.)

'Did you know that Michael and Michael D. go a long way back to Galway?' Ann explained. 'Michael was always speaking for him at Labour Party meetings. Anyway, that's why we were there. To tell the truth, we've been to that Eurovision thing before and it's usually the most awful lot of songs. Then in the middle of it all, when everybody was almost asleep with the boredom, they put this thing on. Did you really like it? Well, it woke the whole place up, I can tell you. It was all anyone could speak about afterwards, and then they carried on about it the next day and the next week. You like it then? I'm glad of that. We were all very proud.'

There is a cynical school of thought that thinks of *Riverdance* as pure hokum. I was in New York for a test screening of *A Midsummer Night's Dream* two years later (after it had been acquired for the US by Miramax) and the full-blown *Riverdance* show derived from the original seven-minute filler was about to open at the Radio City Music Hall. The buzz about the show was electric, and its unabashed ambition seemed to be the fusion of what was claimed to be a uniquely Celtic music and dance with other forms from around the world. I thought it was a curate's egg, but its ambition was beyond reproach, and its achievement in reviving a nearly defunct local dance form to the point of full-scale world admiration was momentous. Many people out there still wanted a song and dance show, and this marked the beginning of a new era for the form.

After the test screening I spent a couple of hours alone in one of the many Irish bars in New York, drinking Guinness and listening to U2 playing 'Sunday Bloody Sunday'. I could see, just for a moment, the appeal of being an Irishman in New York, but I could also see more than anything that *Riverdance* had pumped up the blood of every man and woman claiming Irish descent from New Jersey to Oakland. It was the most glorious piece of Irish propaganda ever perpetrated on the people of the world.

It is no exaggeration to state that the original seven-minute routine was a defining moment in the emergence of the new Ireland, and even now it sends electric waves up my spine. It started off predictably enough with an Enyaesque highly produced, plaintive solo female voice, underscored by a ghostly chorus. Then Jean Butler emerged on to the stage and her long legs instantly began the redefinition of Irish dance, as she perfectly melded its peculiar dead-arm style with the athleticism of a ballet dancer. Then the troupe of bodrun bashers struck up a series of mighty and rapid blows, and Michael Flatley hurtled on to the stage like an Irishman whose night class in flamenco had been cancelled halfway through but who was determined to have a craic anyway.

Their duet was the footstomping proof that Irish dancing was no longer the embarrassing, sexless cousin of Morris dancing in England. Flatley defied all the conventions, with his arms flexing above his head, and, confronting Jean Butler's straight-backed elegance, her deer-like grace, appeared to be performing some ancient Irish mating ritual from the lost time of the High Kings. At about this point in the videotape I begin to twitch. I can't Irish dance, and our floorboards would give way if I tried, but my fingers begin to click, my feet begin to glide and my mind is yearning for the entrance of the big chorus of dancers. On they come, first one row, all dressed in black, Irish hair and breasts bouncing all over the place, and then the second rank. And then my favourite camera move in TV history, as the two principals and the two rows become one long row and the camera tracks from stage right to stage left along dozens of pairs of jumping, kicking, stomping feet. The music climaxes, Flatley and Butler dance front stage again, the music stops. And then comes the micro-second.

It's the tiniest moment of silence, a synapse. The audience have just realised that someone has taken their country's potentially absurd dance form and transformed it from bottom of Division Three to outright champions in the Premier League – in just seven minutes. In that tiny moment you know they can't believe it. And then they roar. It's a roar that says, 'We always said we were as good as everyone else, and we are. Jesus, maybe we're even better.' It is a roar of national pride, the ecstasy of a people whose stagecraft and self-belief have finally, after hundreds of years of bullshit and boasting born from persecution and criticism, become one before their eyes. It was not a bellicose roar, it was a roar of hope fulfilled. It makes my eyes leak every time I hear it.

That's what I watched, again and again, the Saturday night I met my sister Maeve for the first time. The sixth time round Benjamin woke up, and I danced him back to sleep on my shoulder, his deeply taken breaths undisturbed by his father's insane, elemental excitement beneath him. In Ireland the Sunday papers were going to press on more stories about the abandoned love children of Catholic bishops, about headteachers exposed as serial child molesters and supermarket owners filling the pockets of politicians with filthy lucre. Dancing out the old, dancing in the new.

In another life this book too could have had another name. It might have been christened *The Moses Syndrome*. This

prophet of Judaism, Islam and Christianity was a stranger
in a strange land, one who after a few minutes on the at-
risk register in the bulrushes was adopted and raised by an
Egyptian princess from the enemy camp. Moses is the big
one of the adopted.

In a way that I would have entirely endorsed as a
teenager, Moses rebelled against his new land, claimed
to be the mouthpiece of God, and set about telling everyone else what to do. In a way that partially reflects my
own experience of adoption, he mistrusted all ortho-
doxies and fought to get new ground rules tested and
agreed. He was an awkward bastard too, taking it upon
himself to smash the first set of Commandments, boor-
ishly forcing the Lord back to his chisel, rather like my
Irish trade union leader father. Was I an occasionally
fervent opponent of injustice because of the awkward-
squad gene flowing through me, or was it because I had
the Moses Syndrome?

The dreadfulness of this title, quite apart from inciting
the toughs in business class to expect a thriller in the vein
of *The Andromeda Strain* or *The Satan Bug*, was that it also
had a quasi-mystical sect feeling to it, as if He (Moses) was
the first of Us – the brethren of the adopted. When in fact
He and his moral order was, it turns out, one of the main
factors in messing it up for Us in the first place. Ironically
it was because of Moses that I was revisiting my Ten
Commandments in the Book of Exodus, in the second of
which I unexpectedly found the inspiration for my title:

'Thou shalt not make unto thee any graven image or any likeness of any thing.'

'Likeness'. That was my word, a word that sustained many of the meanings I wanted my title to bear. Likeness as in 'alikeness', of course, as in how astonishingly alike I was to this family of complete Irish strangers. Yet perhaps it was only 'a good likeness' in that, like a well-made police photofit, the resemblance might be astonishing but there were still marked differences in shading and depth. There was also the double positive implied in the title, and I wanted this, because for the mass audience, especially in American movies-of-the-week and British soaps, the return of an adopted child has all too often been utilised as a plot device for a 'bad seed' story. Which is absurd, because adopted people have spent their lives getting along with and loving those who there was no natural reason for them to know. There is no category of people more highly trained in the art of compromise and reconciliation than the adopted. But most of all, when I decided to write this book I made a vow. I would tell the story in a true likeness of the events as they happened.

The difficult truth is that I now found myself, as the heat of summer began to fade, standing at a door I would have rather not entered. Thus far there perhaps had been two points at which I could have gone to the parents I had always known and told them what was going on. Theoretically, I could have gone at the very outset, when-ever that was, and I could have gone after meeting Ann and Michael for the first time. The truth is that I didn't want to endure what I feared would be a negative reaction at either stage, when it was obvious to me that while there was still so much to be discovered it was not completely certain that I might not suddenly want to throw the whole process into reverse gear. I wanted to spare my parents' feelings, and in truth I also wanted to protect myself from the inevitable strength of their reaction. This might be seen as cowardly, but I believe it to be the opposite. In order to insulate these epic days from any forces of opposition, I was prepared to reap a harsher harvest later on.

This conscious decision not to tell my parents at two early stages denied us all the opportunity to know if they might have reacted differently in the end if they had been included along the way. The difficulty with my effort to heap blame upon myself is that if, as they claim, they know me well then it is also true that I know them too. Some adoptive parents are made for mediation and counselling and soul-bearing and guidance and mutual support groups and working with their children as equals. My parents, I knew, did not subscribe to any of these things. I was a son with an infinite sense for finding the grey areas in any issue, while they were people who believed in the fundamental right to think in black and white. I respected that right, but in this, the greyest period of my entire life, I believed I had a right to keep black and white out of it for a period of time of which I could be the only judge.

The Anglican *Book of Common Prayer* has a particular set of prayers to be said 'on the first day of Lent or at other times as the ordinary shall appoint'. These prayers are a Communation, or a Denouncement of God's anger against sinners. Each line begins: 'Cursed is he . . .' The first line is the cousin to the commandment about graven images: 'Cursed is the man that maketh any carved or molten image to worship it.' The second line proclaims: 'Cursed is he that curseth his father or mother.' And all answer amen.

My greatest inner conflict in dealing with my parents was my own disease of moderation in all things. It made it impossible to truly understand that any parent would feel justified in allowing their own anger and upset to dominate the evident happiness of their child in circumstances such as these. I felt that both in my parents' lives and in the lives of my newly found natural parents I had always brought blessings, not curses.

Alas, this was not so. It was my fate that the way in which I told my parents about having found Ann and Michael was to become a textbook case of what not to do. One afternoon I drove the few miles to the fringes of north Kent. I had spent much of the previous week asking my closest friends how the hell I was supposed to go about this, and out of these consultations and my own folly I constructed what I had been brought up to know as 'a white lie'. I gave my parents a more or less precise summary of the story that has gone before with one bald untruth – I said that it was not I who had contacted the Brennans, but they who had

contacted me. I had discovered in my researches that a
natural parent equipped with a date, sex and place of their
child's birth could, with help and endurance, correlate the
truncated birth certificates in the Adopted Children's
Register with the long-form birth certificates sufficiently
to get to a handful of likely candidates. The rest could be
done by private detectives.

My father, having spent his life in motor insurance
sifting truth from lies in thousands of accident and theft
claims, believed this for about five seconds. So, cata-
clysmically, instead of having what would have been a
pained but eventually positive discussion about what had
actually happened, we had a furious row about what had
not happened. This lay unresolved for the rest of his life.
I had a great deal of affection for my father, and a deeper
appreciation of the frustrations of his life than he ever
would have thought possible from one younger than
himself, but when Lydia, in an act of true valiance, drove
down to them herself a few weeks later her olive branch
was snapped in the face of unabated fury. In a later phone
call she was said to have 'been sent to do my dirty work'.
I was mystified as to how someone who was so obviously
a peacemaker could be described in such terms, and something in me began to give way.

A few months later Lydia produced the ultimate olive
branch – a pair of girl twins, Sasha and Tara. This we
thought would give us all an opportunity to mend our
differences – new life, twice over, female, beautiful. Twice

I asked my parents if they would like to come to see the girls, but they never did. They would have come, I feel sure of that, in the end, but for my father the opportunity was gone. Within two more months he had died. At the funeral the vicar had been fed an ill-judged line referring to him as a devoted grandfather to our two boys, and to Sasha and Tara 'who were not seen'. I honestly think that others in my position then would have stood up and said, 'How much more of this shit do I have to put up with?' But I didn't. I played black sheep for the rest of the day. When a definitively un-Christian card arrived from a godmother I hardly knew a week later, berating 'the suffering you caused your father in the months before his death', I just sighed and pushed it deep into the kitchen bin.

Soon after this, I spoke to a greatly respected friend who is in his eighties, about the unhappy events involving my family and me in my adoption quest. He is a man of good judgement, great experience and fierce independence of mind. Having considered the matter he said, 'On balance, I think you had no other course than to behave as you did in this matter. The worst you could be accused of is a degree of disloyalty, but it is hard to conceive how you could have avoided it.' Now, half a decade later, my mother is enormously fond of Sasha and Tara, and they of her, and things are back on an even keel. It must have been awful for her to have to deal almost simultaneously with the shock of a son tracing his natural parents and the death of her husband, but she dealt with it with great resilience and courage.

My adoptive brother, who is five years older than me, still lives at home with my mother, and they value each other's companionship enormously. The home the two still live in is, when I return with the children for Sunday lunch, a magical repository of sense memories – light aircraft droning over Biggin Hill, the chime of the grandfather clock, wood pigeons cooing, the white of the wall against which I kicked a ball thousands of times. It is a home where two hardworking parents gave everything they had to raise two adopted sons. Although I left that nest, raised my own family and traced the mother who gave me away three decades ago, I do not feel any less grateful to my adoptive parents. I know that tracing my birth parents caused them much unhappiness, but nobody can take away from them that although they were not my biological parents, they were still my mum and dad.

9

Hi Ho Silver Lining

To CONJURE the wonder of a wedding is as difficult as writing about Christmas. Both are full of ritual, recitation and, from above, seem homogenous. The definition of a successful wedding or Christmas Day is that everything has gone to plan, that any incidents passing into family folklore later originate from happiness not disaster.

Maeve's wedding was special, something out of the ordinary. At centre stage was a young woman carrying the beginnings of another life whose own life had been terribly threatened just over a year before. By her side was a man of oak, Lar, who'd been intimately involved in both processes – the quintessence of the quietly spoken, measured, mature-beyond-his-years hero. This was their day, and I am extraordinarily fortunate that a second videotape from Ireland allows me to rewitness this day too, a wedding video produced by my youngest brother, Shane.

Although it's clear that Maeve and Lar were the absolute stars that day, my own role was more than a walk-on, and on the video I stick out like a sore thumb, especially in the church. I am the one (unaware that he is on tape) who doesn't close his eyes for prayers but just sits there with an enormous stupid grin on his big head. I am the one who doesn't go up for communion but gawps at everyone else's obeisance. And I am the one who keeps turning up from behind a tree as the Brennan family assembles for group photographs into which, to the mystification of many onlookers, I have become a central figure. Some know who I am, others think I am the 'friend from London', and one or two are beginning to scratch their heads saying, 'Who's the fella in the pinstripe suit? Isn't he awful like Michael as a young man?'

But my story of Maeve's wedding began the day before. Before I could attend there was still a considerable chunk of outstanding business to be executed, in particular meeting two more brothers. This is quite a challenge to put upon the shoulders of a family at the quietest of times, but the day before their sister's wedding was about as intense a moment as could have been chosen. The family home was buzzing with Maeve and her pre-nuptial entourage, so Lydia and I were collected from the airport by Michael and taken to the hotel where we were staying, the West County in Chapelizod, a mile from both the house and the church.

My difficulty with the narrative of the rest of the day, and the weekend, is that the drinking seemed to start at lunchtime on the first day and go on until we left two days later. Ann already knew that I had the liver of a baby sparrow and gave Liam a stern pre-match talk on how he was not to go trying to pour drink down my throat. I think he did his best to follow this edict, but the night before a wedding was not an easy moment for him to embrace the code of a teetotal. I mention this because what I remember about Liam was not a first handshake, or even a first meeting, but a first moment when our relationship was suddenly switched on, when we found ourselves alone at the hotel bar at about seven o'clock in the evening.

It was then that I realised that Liam was not troubled about his brother's return from exile mainly because he barely had a spare moment in his life to switch his attention away from the demands of the day. He was too busy to indulge in retrospectives. He and Anita lived at a constant eighty miles an hour in the fast lane, working their socks off, he as an electrical contractor, she as a caterer, surrounded by their own children and by Anita's family. Their leisure, too, was lived at a pace, Liam still training and playing left-back in a football team, and Anita becoming increasingly politically active. They were utterly committed to the new Ireland, and were typical of the emerging middle class that was choosing to send its children to Irish-speaking schools. They had clear views, and the appearance of an Irish illegitimate from the beginning of the 1960s was no surprise, caused no worries, and was to be accepted as a matter of fact not a cause for navel-gazing.

So Liam and I did not have the all-embracing discussion I'd had with Maeve, or the great historical debates I would go on to have with Barry. Instead we talked about what we both enjoyed talking about, which was soccer. Within a pint we had laid on the table the naked prejudices we both held about the other's soccer worth. I argued that in England we thought the Irish soccer team a joke because only two of them had Irish accents, that in any case they were all a bunch of dirty, scything foulers, and that (other than Poland) they were the one team in the world we could most depend upon to bollocks it up for us, doing all they could to spoil our game purely because they hated us so much.

Liam put his glass down and countered that the Irish team weren't born in Ireland because their pure Irish parents had all been driven to seek work on the mainland because of the legacy of English rule. As far as ability was concerned, he mentioned the name of George Best and asked if I could name a better English player in the game's history (I could not). And dealing with my final point, he said that of course they couldn't stand us – how did we feel about the Germans?

My eyes opened wide. 'The Germans,' I spluttered. 'We've had two wars and an economic defeat against them this century. Of course we hate the Germans.'

'That's how we feel about England,' said Liam.

'You're joking, aren't you?' I went on. 'Come on, if it was England against Germany in the World Cup Final, who would you rather won?'

Liam didn't hesitate. 'Germany, of course.'

Liam is a man of his word. Four years later England were playing Argentina in the quarter-finals of the World Cup, yet another match that left a scar in the heart of every Englishman. I was on a trip to Dublin at the time, staying with Ann and Michael, and Benjamin, who was then six, was with me. The whole family sat in front of the television as the game evolved from one climatic moment to another, the teams level after extra time and the outcome to be decided by a penalty shoot-out. Benjamin and I watched in amazement as Liam and his boys cheered each and every Argentinian penalty success, saving their mightiest hurrah for the moment when David Batty missed for England, leaving us Anglo-Saxons with another bitter taste of the what-might-have-beens. If Benjamin had the power of arrest he would have clapped handcuffs on the lot of them and given them a dose of the treatment meted out to Lord Haw-Haw.

After the football discussion on the night before Maeve's wedding, the evening begins to go fuzzy at the edges. I remember being introduced to some of Liam's friends as 'me brother' and wondering if they had all known this already, or if this really was the point of first revelation. If it was, they all dealt with it very well, though how they were processing the difference in accents between Lord Haw-Haw and Lord Snooty I am less certain. It all became more complicated when the throng was joined by sisters-in-law, girlfriends, Maeve and some of her oldest friends

(many of whom had flown in from around the world), and
Lydia was asked who she was and how she came to know
Maeve and Lar. She was so confused as to who did and did
not know about me that she eventually said, 'I'm not certain
which version I'm meant to give, so can I just tell you to
ask my husband, but I'm extremely pleased to be here
anyway.'

Also in the bar of the hotel that night was Shane. If I sat
up on a bar stool and he stood on the floor it was possible
for me to look him in the eye, but his spectacular height
otherwise meant that he could have used me as a tripod for
his camera. The night before the wedding he was superbly
professional, having done a reconnaissance of the church
during the rehearsal to check his camera angles, and he
arrived in the bar with that brisk air of someone who has
just come from work. But of all the children, Shane, despite
his height, was the most obvious candidate to have been
the kid brother. He was soft-spoken (though not squeaky
like mid-period Barry), a gentle man with a gentle mind,
very close to both parents, still with his life interwoven with
both of theirs. He was also ambitious, though, and even in
his early twenties clearly had an iron business fist lurking
in the velvet glove. He also had a driving style that he
seemed to have inherited from Michael, very firm but, even
in his home city, not always exactly certain which turning
to take next. Benjamin and I, conversely, were both born
with the spatial apparatus of a homing pigeon, and I've
found myself being driven in Dublin by both Michael and

Shane saying, 'Er . . . isn't it a left here?' and them saying,
'Do you know, I think you're right. Isn't that an amazing
thing altogether?'

But what I most wondered about was the complexity of
the fact that we had both ended up doing the same kind of
work for a living. On the surface the fact that we had both
gone into television, even though we knew nothing of each
other's existence, might lend credence to the idea that in
our nature we were similarly made, destined to follow
similar courses, yet this is nowhere near the truth. Shane
had left school and gone straight onto a media training
course, his ambition and his path one and the same. At his
age I had wanted to be a writer and dramatist, but found
myself in such financial difficulty that I went into journalism to pay the bills, which led almost by accident into
arts television. On my first day in TV I was given a pile
of VHSs of past transmissions to watch and I didn't even
know how to work the video player. Shane, at the age I
entered journalism, was operating live studio cameras at
RTE, the Irish state broadcaster. I now know how to do
that kind of stuff, but it took me years to learn. I am from
the last generation of the amateur in broadcasting. Shane
is from the first generation of the media studies, dyed-in-
the-wool professionals. One day we will do something
together as equals.

One of the saddest things about growing up is going to bad
weddings. I longed for a wedding day as much as any

teenage girl, and when it came to the moment that I gave my vows a quiver of shivers shot up my spine. Much of the rest of the day exhausted me, but we were blessed that we'd both meant it in church. I've been to many weddings now where concerned guests fret like worried dogs saying, 'I'll give it five years,' and now I'm in my late thirties I've seen that too often they've been proved right. If you have a sensitive bone in your body, you can always tell. And you know the in-laws can tell too, that what they are paying for is not so much a love match as a transaction. I'd hoped my generation had got past all this; it hasn't.

The in-laws at Maeve and Lar's wedding could hardly wipe the smiles off their faces, and if there is a more jovial pair of speeches than those given by the two fathers-in-law I'd like to see them. Michael's speech was a cracker, drawing on all his experience as a political orator. Typical of his approach was his pairing of a joke about Maeve's vegetarianism, advising Lar to finish his plate because that was the last square meal he was likely to see in some time, with a tribute to the principle behind her vegetarianism, almost apologising for having attempted to make her eat meat as a teenager and for his failure then to recognise that she was acting not on a fad but out of conviction.

The wedding ceremony itself had been the antithesis of those weddings of acquaintances where one just prays for it to be over. I could have sat through this one a hundred times. At the wonderful reception at the Marine Hotel on the coast north of Dublin I had four seminal moments. The first came half an hour or so after we'd arrived, as we were preparing to go through to the dining room. I'd lost Lydia for a moment, and was happily gazing out at the sea, when Michael came past with his speech notes in his hand.

'Are you all right there, Paul?'

'I'm great. Lydia's gone to the loo.'

'Well, I'm glad I got you alone for a moment. I'm a pretty busy guy today but I figured you were big enough to take care of yourself.'

'I am, and I've managed to avoid the mouth-almighty.' This was a reference to a legendary family busybody, about whom I was forewarned.

'Well, you've done well enough there all right, but don't get complacent because she's the kind of woman who's likely to leap out at you from behind a bush. Anyway, listen, Ann and I are overjoyed that you're here today. I'm sorry that some people know and some people don't, it's just that it's been a big thing telling for us, a very big thing. Maybe we could have gone a bit quicker, but they'll all know soon.'

'Don't worry, I'm fine. It's your business. Anyway, I'd rather not have been the centre of attention. This is Maeve's day.'

'That's how I figured it, too. You know, I was thinking about it the other day. It comes down to this. You were adopted because of the Catholic Church. But you were not aborted because of the Catholic Church. I think that's quite a thought altogether.'

Which it was, and not exactly light banter at a wedding

reception either. And not the way I looked at it, or ever would. But that was the way it was in 1961, and 1971 and 1981 and 1991 and 2001, so long as there was a Catholic Church sitting in judgement on sex outside of marriage. There were 175,000 abortions in the UK last year, and the Irish now swell these numbers, flying in to abort and flying out same day. Have they exchanged one bloody mess for another?

My second seminal moment came when I took to the dance floor with Ann after supper and all I had to offer was my mid-seventies 'Hi Ho Silver Lining' freestyle. She, I liked to think, had already gained heaps of joy from seeing how her first born had turned out, but she could not conceal her horror at my untrained feet. Here was a woman, a colleen, with every step at her command, all the orthodox foxtrots and waltzes, and all the shin-kicking, arms-dangling Irish ones too. And there was First Born, like an extra in a porn movie, just sort of gyrating. I think she felt more guilt in that moment than at any time in the preceding three decades.

The problem was, of course, that where the other children had been taught Irish dancing, in England I had been doing Ironic dancing. It started at university in 1980, that insincere gazing at the work of your own feet, the striking of pained poses, that non-dancing. It worked very well with Joy Division or Elvis Costello, but to a showband playing the theme tune from *Notting Hill* at a wedding it just seemed as if I was a black hole on the dance floor, taking space but making no joy.

I was delighted then to escape the dance floor, when I was led off for my third seminal moment by Barry, to the quiet and elegant little bar away from the main action. For there, waiting for us, with four Irish whiskeys lined up on the bar, were Liam and Shane.

Liam may be a man of few words, but he knows what to do with them. 'All right there, now . . . listen, will you take a glass of whiskey with us because Mam came out with some bollocks about you not drinking very much but as far as I can see you haven't stopped since yesterday.'

I laughed. 'I will, Liam. And I don't drink spirits – except I do drink whiskey.'

'Ah, that's great now. Do you want some of that there water stuff in it?'

'Fuck off.'

'That's the spirit. Anyway, maybe this is the kind of thing the father should be saying, but I reckon with us four brothers standing all together for the first time it's down to me. Shane, Barry, lift up your glasses. And let's drink a toast to our brother, Paul.'

I faced three beaming smiles, three generous faces, three young men who'd plotted this moment. And I loved them for it. I downed mine in one.

'Right,' I said, 'my round. Who's for another one?'

Liam looked delighted, as if a priest had just given him a look of his *Playboy*. 'You want another one?'

'I do, and I'm buying.'

Liam smiled broadly. 'Well, I'll have the same again.'

For the first time my younger brother and I were talking the same language.

A couple of hours later the guests made their way to a fleet of minibuses that were to take them back to various points in Dublin. I staggered on board with Lydia's assistance and sat by her side on a double seat. A few moments later two men in their late fifties or early sixties staggered on and sat in the double seat in front of us. Lydia and I could see only the backs of their heads but we both thought the same thought instantly. 'These two men have got exactly the same head as Benjamin.' I turned to Barry, who was sitting a couple of seats away, and asked who they were.

'Ah, they'd be Dad's brothers.'

He was about to tell me more when one of them started to sing, beautifully, and for the duration of the journey, with the whole minibus joining in with the choruses. Now I saw, like a stranger peeking through a keyhole, the thing I'd heard of and had not believed existed. It was the craic, and in England it does not exist. In my unknowing childhood I would have wished that it had, even though I did not know what it was.

10

A False Stop

ACCORDING to the old chroniclers of Ireland, the stories were classified into prim-sceil (chief tales) and fo-sceil (minor tales). These were sub-divided. The prim-sceil were: 1. battles; 2. voyages; 3. tragedies; 4. adventures; 5. cattle-raids; 6. military expeditions; 7. courtships; 8. elopements; 9. concealments; 10 destructions; 11. sieges; 12. feasts; 13 slaughters. The fo-sceil were: 1. pursuits; 2. visions; 3. exiles or banishments; 4. lake eruptions.

The Brehon Laws, the ancient law system of Ireland, stipulated that only qualified story-tellers could recite these sagas and tales. To be able to tell both chief and minor tales one had to have achieved the four top degrees available at bardic schools . . . With the suppression of the bardic schools in the seventeenth century by the English, the old oral tradition of story-telling was taken up by the seanchai, which word has come down in English as seannachie. It was stipulated in ancient law that a qualified story-teller should know at least two hundred prim-sceil and one hundred fo-sceil.[*]

The news from Ireland is of a totally different order today than that of only a decade ago. If ever I had a pipe dream of moving there I can now forget it. Property prices are higher than in most parts of London. The time to have moved there would have been when my adoption quest came to fruition. Today the west is full of Germans, Dutch, Japanese and rich Irish buying up land where potatoes once rotted in the field. The hunger today is for green wilderness within a short drive of a golf course.

This caused me some real heartache. I still didn't seem to be able to love my mother country. Perhaps love of location is like love of a person, maybe you can only fall in love properly three times, and after that new love is a shadow of what once went before. At fourteen I saw the Alps for the first time, in Switzerland, Austria and Italy. At their base, on Lake Garda, I saw these ubermenschen tourists in Volkswagens, bathing their tanned bodies and dancing to Donna Summer's 'I Feel Love'. Nothing like this existed in England. At fifteen I saw Mycaenae and a sunset at Cape Sounion, heard crickets in the olive trees, ate a shish kebab

---

[*] Peter Beresford Ellis, *A Dictionary of Irish Mythology*, Constable, 1987.

by the vast trench of the Corinth Canal, and fell in love. And at eighteen I travelled down the valleys of the Soane and the Rhone and at last reached the azure Mediterranean at Marseilles, where white stone churches were pock-marked with the stain of German shrapnel that exploded thirty-five years before.

What could I see in the country that bore me now my eye was already beguiled by other far greater places, even in Europe? The summer after Maeve's wedding Lydia and I filled the car with children, including Sasha and Tara, who were now two months old, and headed for Dublin for a happy stay with Ann and Michael. We travelled across North Wales to Holyhead. To our left for nearly two hours were the mountains of Snowdonia. They were magnificent, yet I was disappointed that I just knew they had no match in Ireland, despite what I had been told by an army of Eirephiles.

That summer's trip was glorious, and especially for the children. Jake and Benjamin went to stay at Liam's house with Finian and Donnacha and thus acquired something I had never had – some proper cousins. And Ann and Michael (and Shane, who was like a patron saint with babies) looked after Sasha and Tara as we went with the boys to Galway City. There we stayed at the Great Southern Hotel, with its rooftop pool with a view of the Aran Islands, and drove through Tuam, where Michael had grown up and first went to work at the local sugar beet factory. Back in Dublin, Liam and Anita took us out to dinner in Temple

Bar, then flickering into life, now superior to Covent Garden as an example of inner city revival based on filling rotting old buildings with fashionable clothes and food. And we went shopping at Arnott's department store, which has always amused me. Barry now plays occasionally for my fat football team and the Dublin team shirt he wears is sponsored by and has written across its front 'Arnott's'. Every time I see him wearing it, it looks like fate's ultimate visual pun.

But the world has become so homogenous. The house in Palmerstown was nearly identical to the house in Bromley where I had the happiest days of my childhood. Everywhere we went in Ireland was by road, every town we visited had the same brand names as in England. It was even possible for me to poison my system more thoroughly than at home with chocolate, for Dublin was used as a market testing area by Cadbury's and was years ahead of us with many tooth-rotting treats. Maeve took Lydia and me and the boys on a tour of the under-rated county of Meath, with its Neolithic burial chambers at Newgrange and the ancient meeting spot for the High Kings (and supposedly the point where St Patrick converted the Irish to Christianity) at the Hill of Tara. In that whole summer trip, that was the only moment where I came near to sensing some essence of Ireland. Other than the ever expanding suburbs, I had seen only grey, reflecting water, or poorly soiled, rocky western fields, which were living proof that emigration was the only option in the past for many reasons other than the harshness of English rule.

What I could not do was connect. A year or so on, nearing yet another birthday under the autumn sky in south London, this failure was actually beginning to gnaw at me. Some men I know still seem to have the gall to announce to their wives and children that they are off to walk in the Andes for a fortnight, but I do not have the constitution or the desire to leave those I love most dearly at a time when I believe they need me. However my craving to head off into some part of Ireland on my own was now reaching a breaking point. I was better gone for a few days. All I needed was an excuse.

It came in the form of a coincidence. I had hoped to go walking the Twelve Bens in Connemara in a group organised by a friend, but the planning for this went awry, leaving me with a credit for a Ryanair return flight. And in London, among commissioning editors of television drama, the hunt was on for the next great novel adaptation. I had come across Anthony Trollope's first novel, *The Macdermots of Ballycloran*, by accident, and read it with astonishment. To the English reader, Trollope had been the supreme chronicler of personal, political machinations in nineteenth-century cathedral closes, and his continuing appeal rested on the continuing existence of identical patterns of behaviour in the law, the church, universities, the civil service, everywhere where men who made nothing came together with a thirst for self-promotion concealed within a carapace of concern for the common good. In *The Macdermots*

Trollope's timing had been almost journalistic. He described the rapacious hunger of many in Ireland who were living on the margins of existence, and just one month after he had finished it in 1845 the first news of the potato blight was announced.

Trollope had written the book when he was working as Surveyor's Clerk for the Central District of Ireland, stationed in County Offaly (then King's County) at Banagher, a port on the Shannon. Through this posting he came to understand the peculiar dilemma of the Irish Catholic gentry, who were not handling money well on their own account but were also holed beneath the water line by the long years of confiscations and penal laws that had robbed them of their lands. He was also writing at a time when the language of Irish was losing ground to English, and he managed to capture dialogue that was accurate in the extraordinary sentence constructions of a people in the process of assimilating one language on top of another, while entirely avoiding the patronising depiction of the stage Irishman.

But I loved the book because of its beginning, because both Trollope and his narrator were inspired to tell the tale by a walk in the Irish countryside. Somehow, this Englishman had walked the Irish earth and been inspired. Chapter One opens thus:

> In the autumn, 184–, business took me into the West of Ireland, and, amongst other places, to the quiet little

village of Drumsna, which is in the province of
Connaught, County Leitrim, about 72 miles W.N.W.
of Dublin, on the mail-coach road to Sligo. I reached
the little inn there in the morning by the said mail,
my purpose being to leave it in the evening by the day
coach; and as my business was but of short duration,
I was left, after an early dinner, to amuse myself. Now,
in such a situation, to take a walk is all the brightest
man can do, and the dullest always does the same.
There is a kind of gratification in seeing what one has
never seen before, be it ever so little worth seeing; and
the gratification is the greater if the chances be that
one will never see it again . . .

After proceeding a mile or so, taking two or three
turns to look for improvement, I began to perceive
evident signs on the part of the road of retrograding
into lane-ism; the road had evidently deserted it, and
made for cars and coaches, its traffic appeared to be
now confined to donkeys carrying turf home from the
bog . . .

The usual story, thought I, of Connaught gentlemen; an extravagant landlord, reckless tenants, debt,
embarrassment, despair, and ruin. Well, I walked up
the deserted avenue and very shortly found myself in
front of the house. Oh what a picture of misery, of
useless expenditure, unfinished pretence, and prema-
ture decay . . . The entire roof was off; one could see
the rotting joists and beams, some fallen, some falling,

the rest ready to fall, like the skeleton of a felon left to rot on an open gibet . . . I . . . walked round the whole mansion; not only was there not a pane of glass in the whole, but the window frames were all gone; everything that wanted keeping was gone; everything that required care to preserve it had perished. Time had not touched it. Time had evidently not yet had the leisure to do his work. He is sure, but slow. Ruin works fast enough, unaided, where once he puts his foot. Time would have pulled down the chimneys – Ruin had taken off the slates; Time would have bulged the walls – Ruin brought in the rain, rotted the timbers, and assisted the thieves. Poor old Time will have but little left in him at Ballycloran.

I had learned it was possible that the house Trollope himself had seen as a ruin in Drumsna in the 1840s was still standing today. If ever an adaptation of the novel were to be commissioned it seemed crucial that I should have seen it. It could be a wasted trip, or it could provide divine inspiration, but I could not fail to seek it out at all. I rang up Ryanair and booked my tickets. At last I had a journey to Ireland planned that was looking not into my own but into someone else's past.

When I flew in to Dublin nobody was there to meet me, which was precisely what I wanted. I hired a car, bought some snacks, and sat in the car park for a few minutes with a map of Ireland. It was approaching twelve noon, so I switched on the radio to find some news. From out of the speakers came not a dry voice in current affairs but the tolling bells of the Angelus that RTE Radio still broadcasts every morning and evening, marking the call to prayer. I closed my eyes and let this wash over me, as I had years before with the mullah's cry at the mosque next to the American Colony Hotel in Jerusalem. Yet again that paradox, that Ireland was a dripping north European country with a Mediterranean sun-dried heart.

At the news-stand in the airport they'd been selling tapes too, and I'd seen a discounted recording of the original music from *Riverdance*. I slipped it into the tape machine, switched on the engine and headed into the west. My first stop was to be Galway City again, because all the many enthusiasts for Ireland I met, in whom I had confided my loveless marriage with Ireland, kept saying that I should go to Connemara. I had booked into the Great Southern Hotel on the phone from London, but I'd been too smart for my own good in negotiating the price down, insisting that in November I would not pay more than £55 per night. My reward was that instead of the lovely high-ceilinged room I had stayed in with Lydia and the boys I scored a top floor, in the eaves, garret with a tiny window. Worse, the salesman who'd checked out that morning was All-Ireland Fag Smoking Champion, and every molecule of air, carpet, eiderdown, curtain and towel stank of rancid tobacco. After about a minute, so did I.

Night was falling and I was still seeking, yearning with a desire to feel that this was my country, even for a fraction of a second. I got back in the car and drove a couple of miles out of Galway City to Salthill, its seaside resort. I parked and walked along the beach looking out to sea, but it seemed like nothing. As a student I had gone down to the sea in November at Exmouth many times, and I had felt its bitter cold, its raw force. I would always return home invigorated. But the Atlantic at Salthill refused to give me anything back, and the two women I saw walking their dogs in the dusk on the beach seemed to have the weight of the world on their shoulders. Even a child there with his father seemed unsure of this place, wondering why he wasn't in the warm, centrally heated comfort of home.

I went back to the hotel and swam briefly just before the pool was due to close, but on emerging from the shower in my garret I instantly stank of nicotine again. I switched on the television and ordered a beef sandwich from room service. It arrived, monumental, surrounded by crisps. I ate and then scurried through the chill evening air to the greenish-stone Galway Cathedral (the Cathedral of Our Lady Assumed Into Heaven and Saint Nicholas, built in the sixties), where there were more microphoned mumblings, more rushing in and out of the service, and more distressed-looking people hanging around the main door. I prayed that I might have some kind of revelation in Connemara in the morning, left the church with my spirits marginally lifted, and headed for the bright lights of Galway City.

My timing was terrible. The Druid Theatre was shut up for the winter, Eyre Square, which throbbed with live entertainment in the summer, was desolate, and all the pubs I went into in search of the much vaunted live music were filled with glum faces listening to British and American pop from the jukebox. I phoned home and told Lydia that I was having a terrific time, when what I wanted to do more than anything was be back with her and the children. I switched on the television again, and there was a brave RTE documentary telling of an Irish Civil War massacre of Irish by Irish in a village in Kerry. Michael had told me that as a child he was never told even that there had been an Irish Civil War, the Brits being the sole villains of the peace, and it came as a surprise to him and to his entire generation to learn in the sixties and seventies what had really happened in the fight for the future of an Irish republic. To me, sitting in my tobaccoed-out room, with an Irish newspaper filled with the same stale, spiteful news about corrupt politicians, pederastic priests and the one-foot height difference between Van Morrison and his wife, I felt like Gulliver, not among the Yahoos but among the Lilliputians.

In the morning I swam again to clear my mind of the bad temper of the night before. I spread my map of Ireland on to the bonnet of the car, worked out where to go, and headed north-west into Connemara. I drove and drove until I found the scenery that so many people had raved about in London, the range of low mountains known as the

Twelve Bens and the silvery lakes beneath them. I gazed, I switched on the *Riverdance* music, I walked in some sheep shit, I breathed the air, I stared at the sun breaking through the fast-changing grey clouds, I even took my shirt off in the winter chill. Nothing doing, no catharsis, an emotional so-what. The Bens were too small, had no snow, and no soil. If this really was the land of the Celts then I must have been from the branch that originated in north-western France in Brittany, where every inch of ground moved me just as every inch of ground here seemed godforsaken. If I'd had some onion paste I'd have shoved it into my eyes, I so wanted to cry – nothing came.

I was beginning to give up, and decided that I should look for some lunch. I read in a guidebook that Alcock and Brown had landed near Clifden on the coast at the end of the first ever transatlantic flight from Newfoundland in 1919, some 2,880 miles, and that there was a memorial marking the spot where they came down. I was so desperate for even a fragmentary morsel of meaningful history that I headed towards Clifden, leaving my unconsummated affair with Connemara behind me. I'd done pretty well thus far with my map, and decided to make up my own coastal route into Clifden, departing from the road from Leenane to take in the coastal outpost of Cashleen opposite the island of Inishbofin. My chief desire was to hug the coast as much as possible, to get away from that looming, pint-sized mountain range. When the road bent left away from the sea I decided to take an unmarked road

to the right, which I felt sure must also come out at
Cashleen.

I'd gone about a hundred yards down this road, stone
walls on either side, sheep soaking in their fields, when I
saw that a hundred yards further ahead it dipped slightly.
Within this dip a large puddle had formed, fortified on
either side by an embankment of mud and the stone walls.
I didn't want to dawdle in this puddle, allowing water to
splash up into the engine and soak the spark plugs, so I
pressed my foot to the floor and headed towards the puddle
at about forty miles an hour, checking carefully that there
wasn't a tractor or a sheep coming the other way. Perhaps
half a second before the front wheels hit the puddle's edge
I saw that the puddle had, from where I was sitting, no
visible bottom. One second later I had ploughed into it at
full speed to discover that it did have a bottom, but that it
was about four feet below the surface of the water. The car
stalled instantly, its forward motion arrested by the sheer
volume of the undulating Irish rainwater.

I assessed my position. I was in a mustard yellow Opel
Corsa, in what had appeared to be an ordinary puddle in
Connemara, with water lapping halfway up the windscreen
to the level of my ears on either side of my driving position. Was it possible, I wondered, that beneath Ireland's
deepest puddle there was Ireland's best concealed bog, into
which the Opel was about to sink without trace? This
thought must have taken less than a second, because my
hands were flying to the ignition, the gearstick and the

steering wheel, and my feet to the clutch and the accelerator. If it didn't restart first time I realised it wasn't going to start at all. I would get very wet, very cold, and very unpopular with Hertz. The engine fired and I emerged out of the muddy puddle into the lane like some dark, Irish parody of James Bond in his Lotus Esprit coming up in first on to a sun-kissed beach. I drove on for fifty yards, revving the engine like a madman to warm it up, and came to a halt. Like the village idiot who's just walked into a lamp-post I climbed out of the car and looked back at the scene of this debacle. And like a completely English, late twentieth-century, car-dependent wanker I said aloud 'You'd think somebody would have put a sign up.'

Nevertheless, I had just had my first ever solo Irish adventure and acquired my first ever, all-on-my-own Irish tale to tell. In London, I had realised that my adoption quest thus far had elements of both prim-sceil and fo-sceil, involving numbers 2, 4, 9 and 12 from the former (voyages, adventures, concealments and feasts), and numbers 1 to 3 from the latter (pursuits, visions and exiles). The other categories, cattle-raids and slaughters, I could never satisfy, but I could imagine them. What though, I had wondered in the British Library, was number 4 in the fo-sceil division – a lake eruption? Did my unfathomable puddle count? It was only when I got back in the car with my heart beating, laughing to myself, that I realised that my mood in Galway had been so foul because I had been carrying too heavy a load, had been putting myself through too many hoops. I restarted the car and looked up from the dashboard at the sea and the coast beyond the fields. 'Christ,' I thought, 'this is incredibly beautiful.'

I drove on into Clifden, bought two postcards commemorating Alcock and Brown, and sat in the car writing to Jake and Benjamin to thank them for my birthday presents a few days before. It was a fine-looking town with extraordinary property prices and it felt too affluent to be entirely natural. Indeed, with its cute shop fronts it was so perfect that I felt as if I had wandered onto a film set. So I downed a cup of tea and a sandwich and headed south to the other side of Mannin Bay. I searched the radio frequencies as I drove and settled on a Gaelic-speaking station playing the local music. I didn't understand a word, but it felt a hell of a lot more Irish than the *Riverdance* tape, and it also helped attune my ear for the adventure that awaited me around the corner.

I was following my inner compass by now, and with the sea to the right of me it was pretty hard to get lost. Once again I clung to the coast and took a road down to the water's edge, where there was a prosperous-looking boating club boarded up for the winter. I walked along the strand for a while, and then decided to head back towards the main route back to Galway. Like Oedipus I came to a fork in the road. I now realised that I had come down to the strand along an upper road, but that I could if I wished take the lower road back in the same direction. I pressed on along the lower road for about two hundred yards when a tall man suddenly appeared from a field and stood in the middle of the road ahead carrying a large, red Stop sign. I stopped.

A minute passed, and then five more, and still this man, in the middle of nowhere, and for no obvious reason, was showing me the Stop rather than the Go side of his sign. Presumably there was some kind of roadworks around the corner. I got out of the car and listened, but all that could be heard was the lapping of the sea and the engines of the five cars that were now queuing behind me.

The Stop Man was ten yards ahead but, seeing me out of the car, he sidled up with a friendly grin and said, 'Achmachdosshlachmafoy.'

'Oh, hello,' I said. 'I'm from England.'

'Shtumanaferkerprodfggahiwey, the day is nearly done and waddajavkapum.'

'Yes,' I said, 'it's been beautiful, hasn't it? Are we going to be here long, do you think?'

'Lang, long, achshcmush.'

Like Maeve there was something of Spike Milligan about this man, only this was his beetroot-faced cousin. He looked at the Opel, with its mystifying high-tide mark.

'I doono have a car mysel, shcgrrtkls, is this a good gyytrefedsh?'

'Not bad for a hire car. You know. Is there actually anything happening up there?'

The Stop Man smiled at me. 'Could be.' And he very slowly turned away from me and sidled back off to his former spot ten yards up the road. I got back into the car, and another five minutes passed. I got back out again, and seeing me the Stop Man gave me a happy wave as if I was an old pal who he hadn't seen for a while. But he didn't come closer. I looked back to the car behind. The driver, a woman of about thirty, wound her window down.

'What did he say to you?' she asked.

'I'm not sure, to be quite honest. He seemed to be speaking to me in more than one language.'

'Ach, these people are such complete eejits,' she said, which sounded a sour note I hadn't entirely expected.

'Do you know this road?' I enquired.

'Sure I use it every day.'

'Is there some kind of roadworks?'

'The plain truth is there's probably nothing happening up there at all.'

I sort of sauntered near her car for a bit, absorbing what she had just said, and then sauntered back towards her window.

'What, you mean there might be no roadworks?'

'Oh, they might have been trimming a hedge this morning and they've just left that eejit behind with his Stop sign.'

At about that time the first, magnificent episodes of *Father Ted* were showing in England. I had assumed the idiot non-savant priest Dougal to be a work of fiction, but from what this woman was saying he was alive and well and holding a Stop sign on the lower road on Slyne Head.

I sauntered back to my car, gave it a few minutes of Gaelic FM, and wandered back to the woman behind. We had now been here for twenty minutes. It seemed as plain as the nose on our faces that we were, like the Stop Man, the living definition of a waste of time.

'Can I just ask you,' I said to the woman, 'and sorry to be thick, but you reckon if we just drove past him there would be absolutely nothing in our way?'

'I'd say that's exactly what will happen. What a waste of an afternoon. I have books to mark.'

'You're a teacher?'

'Yes.'

I was resolved now. Meeting this man from the pages of J.M. Synge was fascinating in its own way, but here was a woman from the modern Ireland who needed to get on with her life. I felt like a rookie, English lieutenant posted to the west and deeply insensitive to the ways of the local people, but in my gut my conviction was now that this bloke was an escapee from some asylum who'd helped himself to Galway Corporation Overalls and a Stop sign off a flatbed truck. I started my engine and moved slowly forward until I was up alongside him.

'Look, sorry about this, but it's been twenty minutes. Is there another man up the road with a Go sign?'

'I doono bout that gijrrywaquisle.'

'I hope you won't mind, but I think I'll just nip up a bit further and find out.'

'Thank you, sir, hhuryelccbhut.'

I drove, cautiously at first, around one corner, then another, then another. I drove for three miles with the crocodile of five cars behind me until we hit the R341 and headed south to Galway. It was perfectly apparent that there had not been that day any roadworks, hedge trimming, or even cowpat removal on the lower road, and this man from nowhere had wasted twenty minutes of five people's lives for no apparent reason. Except, for me there was a reason, because sometimes a tale that has no purpose has a meaning in the telling, and in telling this story I realised that I had just met one of the last of the old people of the west for whom the word 'Stop' had not prevented the loss of their language, their way of life and, most of all, their non-linear sense of time.

My near sinking earlier had cheered me up, but the Stop Man actually made me laugh out loud. I was unrecognisable as the depressive who'd left the Great Southern Hotel earlier that day, and I felt as if I was being borne along not just by a sense of direction but for a purpose. Two things had happened, and with a third I knew that day would be complete. Twenty miles further on, the road joined the banks of Lough Corrib, and in the distance I saw a turning to the left that in all probability would run down to the lake's shore. I followed it coming out to a large opening with room to park cars and a jetty out into the lake.

There were no boats, no cars, just an immense stillness. It didn't oppress me now as it had by the Twelve Bens. If it had been summer I would have torn off my clothes and jumped in for a swim. Instead I looked around to check that nobody was about, took off my shirt, lay flat on my front on the damp, dark wooden slats of the jetty, and plunged my right arm up to the shoulder into the freezing water. The shock passed across my shoulders, down my spine to the tips of my toes and back up to my brain. No wonder John the Baptist dunked his flock in the Jordan and in the Sea of Galilee. No element can make the human mind feel so absolved, so alive, and, at last, as I looked across the plane of water, my eye almost at the level of its rippling surface, so connected.

The next day I was due to be at Ann and Michael's house in time for supper, so I checked out early from Tobacco Wharf and traversed Counties Galway and Roscommon until I reached Carrick-on-Shannon. I don't know what roads I had been taking on previous visits to Ireland but I had somehow managed never to see the River Shannon before. I was used to wide rivers across France, and expected the beauty of the Shannon to be yet more hyperbole. I drove across it with no great expectations and stopped on the other side before walking back across the bridge. It was indeed mighty, and wide, and powerful, and busy and a vital resource, and the interconnection between dozens of loughs of varying sizes. My God, I thought, I'm proud of it. And one day I'll hire a boat on it and take the kids and probably get bitten to death by midges, but until then I shall refer to it as the mighty Shannon River with the pride of a plate-lipped Amazonian.

When I reached Drumsna, left off the main autoroute from Dublin to Sligo, I quickly found Taylor's pub, with its faded plaque celebrating the local association with the young Trollope. It was after lunch and there was just one man and the landlady still in the bar. My sense of direction, and my understanding of the literal nature of what Trollope had written about his walk, led me to believe that I needed to walk east from the little town. I asked the landlady if she knew the location of a house that had come to be known as Ballycloran. She did, and she gave me clear directions, then asked, 'What would it be that you are looking for up there?'

I showed her my copy of *The Macdermots of Ballycloran* and said, 'Nothing really. It's just that the author writes so vividly about his walk to this ruined house. I wondered if there could still be anything left of it.'

The landlady smiled warmly. 'So you're having yourself a bit of an adventure, are you? Are you an Irishman yourself?'

'That's a long story.'

'They all are, my love. Well, I hope you find what you're looking for.'

Five minutes later I had crossed the bridge that goes back over the autoroute and was walking up the lane, bearing right, towards the higher land. The lane was a blend of tarmac and mud, winding upwards past the occasional single-storey house. It was quite deserted, and the clear descendant of the lane Trollope had seen with the occasional donkey carrying turf back from the bog a century and a half before. I hate meeting dogs coming along narrow lanes in my direction, but the black Labrador who was approaching me now was an exemplar of wet-nosed affection and curiosity. Twenty yards behind him was his elderly owner, who, like me, would have been considered insanely underdressed for early winter, in his white shirt and ancient corduroys. The English are useless at meeting each other in country lanes, imploding with irritation that they cannot simply ignore close passers-by, and usually emitting a 'Good morning' or 'Good afternoon' with all the warmth of Basil Fawlty. But this old chap was smiling at me from the moment he caught my eye, and was so ethereal in his bearing that for a moment I wondered if I might be encountering someone's ghost.

'You'll be looking for the old house,' he said as if he had just come off his mobile from the landlady.

'Yes,' I said, 'how did you know?'

'We get one or maybe two a year, mostly from America.'

'But how could you tell that I was one of the one or two.'

'Ah, you get to know the signs.'

I wasn't sure why, but inwardly I bloated with pride at being taken for some professor from the Mid-West making a literary pilgrimage. I imagined that the signs he had read were the special intensity of my concentration on the road, my large studious head, and my evident genius for empathy with a place I had not yet seen.

'Yes, I suppose we all look the same,' I said. 'Is it far now?'

'Oh, maybe a minute's walk,' replied the old man. He was looking at me as if I had got the wrong end of the stick, as if he had entirely unintentionally given me some great compliment in which I was now basting with self-satisfaction. He held my gaze, and spoke on. 'I'm not a mind-reader,' he insisted, 'it's because of what you have in your left hand.'

Which was, of course, the Oxford University Press edition of *The Macdermots of Ballycloran*. 'Thank you,' I said, wishing to pass swiftly on, and walked off certain that he was standing there scratching both his Labrador's and his own head, watching me disappear into the distance. I felt that I should hold my chin high and turn back to wave a hearty farewell, but when I did he had gone.

And then I saw it. In a sodden field populated by damp cows, the two massive flank walls of Ballycloran, entirely overgrown by a profusion of deep-rooted ivy, but for which the walls would have fallen down a hundred years before. As an Irishman two generations back I would have been a farmer in Rathvilly, but we don't have many cattle in Lewisham and I have always lacked confidence in discerning a cow from a bull, so this moment somehow lacked the karma I had desired. As I walked up the lane, I discovered two overgrown columns with decayed pediments that would have marked the beginning of the old drive. I clambered tenderly over the overgrown hedge and into the field, which was one quarter grass and three quarters cow pat.

Now I was standing thirty yards away, looking full on to what would have been the front of the old house, but instead there were now just the two flank walls, and in between a jumble of undergrowth, in the middle of which stood a single cow. I walked towards the house, through which one now had a clear view of the Shannon valley, but the nearer I went the more restless the cow appeared to be. She seemed to have formed the impression that she was the new landlord, and with alarming rapidity, from either side of the flank walls, her gang of bovine mates, embittered by their lot at the hand of man, were appearing in numbers. If I let five seconds go by without action I would then be surrounded by cows to the rear and to the sides, with Viscountess Cow in her country house straight ahead of me. Bollocks to Trollope, I thought, he's had his innings. I'm not having my children remember that I perished beneath three tons of dairy on the hoof. And so, making as much noise as I could (just a sort of aghhahhaggh, really) I turned back towards where I had climbed over the hedge and, at last, sprinted flat out on Irish soil (and cow pat).

I've never before thrown a pair of trousers away simply because I thought they were too dirty to wash, but when I reached the car I got a clean pair from my suitcase and ditched the others in a bin in Drumsna. I hadn't known that it was possible to leap rather than clamber over a hedge,

but the top five feet of me had cleared it with Olympian
ease. It was unfortunate about the ten inches of my right
leg that had had to go through rather than over the hedge,
for it was now livid with bramble scratches, which would
soon be bleeding profusely into my socks. As I prepared
to drive away, I saw that from the door of Taylor's pub the
landlady had seen my entire trouser-changing ritual. I got
back out again.

'Did you find the house?' she said.

'I did. Very interesting.'

'You weren't up there long.'

'No. I saw the Shannon and thought I'd come straight
back down for a look.'

'Did you now? Well if you take the next on the left you
can walk right alongside it.'

'Very good,' I said. 'Yes, I think that's what I'll do.'

The trousers I had taken off were dark blue, the ones I
had put on were fawn. I wanted to get out of the landlady's
view before it looked as if I had been shot in the leg, which
was how I came to be walking by an Irish river for the first
time. I looked back up the hill towards where Ballycloran
should have been, but it was obscured by trees on the lower
slopes of the hill. I looked into the fast-flowing water, and
realised that I had taken myself off on some ill-defined,
aimless tour of the land from which I had sprung with only
an obscure novel as my friend.

That was no way to connect. Michael had offered that,
repeatedly, on the phone, in person, in letters, and I had

always avoided the subject. For he had an encyclopaedic knowledge of the burial places of every relative who had gone before him and had seemed certain that to visit these should be one of my priorities as a new Irishman. I had never visited a grave in my life, and until that moment by the Shannon I simply failed to see the point other than for the purpose of a self-indulgent, maudlin day out. I had plunged my arm into Lough Corrib, but the country I connected to then was an unpeopled construct, making a closed circle of what I had imagined about Ireland and what it was to me in that enervating moment. But it was not real.

Three hours later I was back in Dublin, at Ann and Michael's house. 'You know those family graves,' I said to Michael. His eyes lit up. 'I know you've been on about this for a while, but how do you fancy taking me to have a look?'

The next day, in the cemetery above Rathvilly, by my grandparents' graves, the sun heating the valley below, I finally paid my respects.

And in the church at Rathvilly, a year later, Michael and Benjamin sat in a confessional box either side of the wooden partition. 'What's this?' said Benjamin, and pulled the little curtain back, concealing the grille through which priest and subject would whisper. 'Hey, Gramps,' he said, and stuck one of his fingers through the grill into his grandfather's ear. I could see them both, with their doors open to the church, their moon faces laughing with unrestrained joy.

Epilogue

The Information

You can tell a lot about a subject matter by the company it keeps. If you were to browse through the Social Science monograph stacks of a serious library you would find 'Child Adoption' sandwiched between 'Child Abuse' and 'Children's Homes'. The stark reality of adoption in the present day is that, tragically, these three subjects often become interconnected. Recent social history has shown that a child who cannot be placed for adoption at an early age often ends up languishing in a children's home. Once there, they enter the highest risk category in the country of children most likely to be sexually abused by an adult.

Twenty years ago most of us didn't know what a paedophile was. Today the term is notorious. My own direct experience of the subject comes from my children having been pupils at a state-run nursery where the head was discovered to have been convicted of offences against

young persons. He had been free to roam the school because
nobody had ever bothered to check whether he had a criminal record. In the aftermath of his exposure, many parents
listened in shocked disbelief as the local education authority and the local police squabbled over the fact that they
didn't routinely check criminal records because they
couldn't agree whose budget should pay for the procedure.
They continue to squabble now. I hope one day someone
will bang their heads together and get them to co-fund the
development of a piece of information software which will
eliminate the need for a copper and a bureaucrat to sift
through teacher files independently. When that software is
written they can stop procrastinating and take responsible
action to protect the society which pays for them.

The practical exploitation of the new information technology has therefore yet to take off in the realm of child
welfare. It beggars belief, but at the time of writing there is
still no national database which simply lists and correlates
the children awaiting adoption with those who wish to adopt.
Instead, each local authority maintains its own database and,
bar a few exceptions, they never share their data. Meanwhile,
the children in their care become older and ever more difficult to place in an adoptive home. The UK government has
announced that it intends to set up such a national registry.
A chimp could go to PC World today and find the software
to manage this procedure. We shall see what the Home
Office can do. There will be no excuse for failure.

The information age, then, may come to the rescue of

those not yet born whose fate it will be to be adopted, and those yet to discover that they will be unable to create their own biological children. But has it come too late to help the three quarters of a million birth mothers (and fathers), and the children they gave up before 1975? These people do have the beginnings of an information system – the National Contact Register at Southport, located somewhere called Smedley Hydro. However, this system has dual controls. If an adopted adult wants to make contact with their birth parent they may register their details, as may a birth parent also looking to trace their lost child; but only when *both* parties have expressed a desire for contact does Smedley Hydro then put them in touch with each other. If one party alone registers, their letter gathers dust, and the wish to build a bridge across time goes ever unfulfilled.

Much good contact work has been done with the National Contact Register's two-trigger system, but is it enough? We release mass murderers from the Maze prison in the cause of reconciliation, we add the names of men shot as deserters to war memorials in the cause of humanity, and we have apologised to black people in the cause of contrition for the terrible deeds done to them in the era of slavery. Yet we have still not found a way to help the hundreds of thousands of women who gave up a child and who now live with their daily regret. Surely with all this new technology at our fingertips, we should be able to plug Smedley Hydro into a national database – the driving-licence records for example – so that its counsellors can find the address of a

person who is being sought, and do them the simple courtesy of letting them know that someone is looking for them.
No strings, no pressure – just providing the information
that could possibly lead to a reconciliation.

But will this happen? Small lobbying groups of birth
mothers are pushing for it. They have focused on the
government's commitment to a Freedom of Information
Act, but have so far been disappointed and, in all likelihood, they will not achieve much headway until they appeal
to the European Court of Human Rights. It is clear that
significant progress – the monitored flow of the most basic
information – will only come from political pressure. The
difficulty for these birth mothers is that they are a diminishing constituency: the youngest of them is now in her
forties, and as the peak of adoption activity took place over
the forty years before 1975, some of these women are now
nearer eighty or ninety years old. So who cares?

The answer, and the reason for my restating in this epilogue
some of what has gone before, is that the adopted children
should care. Politically, the birth mothers' case has a tragic
flaw – they gave up their children voluntarily – and it is
frequently and conveniently claimed that they have made
their beds and now must lie in them. The only group who
can credibly come to their assistance is the one perceived as
the innocent party. We may not be infants any more, but we
have experienced the consquences of adoption as children
and, no matter how much we might fear it, as adults we cannot
close our eyes to the political role that adoption has

bequeathed us. The birth-mother lobby's pleas for assistance may well go unheeded, so it is we who have been adopted who should fight for a system which harnesses the technology that has transformed so many other aspects of our lives over the past decade, and which will allow information to flow – with caution and counselling, but without impediment.

The alternative of course is to do nothing, and to leave it to Smedley Hydro. I have no political power, no friends in the right places, but I do know that there will be Members of Parliament across all the parties who have been directly involved in adoption, perhaps because they have been adopted themselves, or because they are an adoptive parent or birth parent. And although I have no professional qualifications to advise on adoption practice today or in the future, I can advise from my own experience as one of the pre-1975 generation of adoptees, that this complicated legacy from our recent past should not be left unresolved just because it is difficult to deal with. The man or woman who has the strength to lobby for a change in the law to allow information to flow freely – as it is meant to do in a democracy – will receive a huge outpouring of thanks from those affected by this issue.

I would wish all this to happen. But at the same time, walking side by side with reform, we pre-1975 adoptees should also pay due credit to that forgotten regiment from history – the parents who adopted us. One of the paradoxes of their position in an adoption system which founded itself on severing all links between child and natural mother, is that their own contribution has been totally ignored. The thinking was that they were damned lucky to be given a child, so they shouldn't complain or mention the difficulties involved in bringing up a child that was not biologically their own. Yes, they were lucky, but they also saved three quarters of a million children from growing up in orphanages and, in nearly all cases, gave their child unconditional love; a very great act of charity that has been utterly overlooked. There is currently a debate in England about what statue should take the vacant plinth in Trafalgar Square – I would like to see a triple sculpture of a titanic adoptive mother next to her adoptive child, both welcoming the birth mother. Anyone else like to subscribe?

And finally, what of those adoptees who are now aged between 26 to 86, those children like me of Adoption's Golden Age? It is highly likely that many are still harbouring a secret about this subject. Ten years ago, if I mentioned that I was adopted at a party, the conversation would swiftly move on to something else. Today I mention it, and before the topic of property prices can inevitably raise its head, a man or a woman says, usually publically, *me too*, or *so was my wife*, or *my best friend has just traced her natural mother*. Adoption is therefore more open for discussion now than at any other time in history. Yet how many of us adoptees will confront the ultimate secret – not only of who gave us away, but of what lies within ourselves that will go forever unexplained if we behave as society has dictated in the past, and remain estranged from those who gave birth to us.